# Praise for
## *Turn South at the Next Magnolia*

"In *Turn South at the Next Magnolia*, Nan Graham has managed to capture 'live' many of the nooks and crannies of everyday life in the south of yesterday as well as of today—family, food, fun and more—that keeps insiders as well as outsiders fascinated with this place we call home."

> Clyde Edgerton,
> author of *Lunch at the Piccadilly*
> and *Where Trouble Sleeps*

"I thoroughly enjoyed [Nan Graham's] stories."

> Bailey White,
> author of *Quite a Year for Plums*
> and *Sleeping at the Starlite Motel*

"Bright, witty and warm . . ."

> *St. Petersburg Times*

"*Turn South at the Next Magnolia* is a collection of stories to savor."

> *Winston-Salem Journal*

"I love to hear a writer read her own work. I've been listening to her book on tape in the car. And it's charming. Y'all have to hear Nan Graham."

> Susan Swagler, *Birmingham News*

"[These] Southern stories have various and diversified flavors. Some pieces are sweet, some are sour, some are chilly, but all are delicious."

> *North Carolina Libraries*

# *In a Magnolia Minute*
## Secrets of a Late Bloomer

### NAN GRAHAM

JOHN F. BLAIR, PUBLISHER
WINSTON-SALEM, NORTH CAROLINA

*The paper in this book meets the guidelines
for permanence and durability of the Committee on
Production Guidelines for Book Longevity
of the Council on Library Resources.*

*Cover Image
by Mandy Johnson © 2005 Corporate Canvas LLC*

Library of Congress Cataloging-in-Publication Data

Graham, Nan, 1936-
In a magnolia minute : secrets of a late bloomer / by Nan Graham.
      p.      cm.
ISBN-13: 978-0-89587-317-0 (alk. paper)
ISBN-10: 0-89587-317-6
1.  American wit and humor.  I. Title.

PN6165.G73 2005
814'.6--dc22

2005010442

DESIGN BY DEBRA LONG HAMPTON
COMPOSITION BY THE ROBERTS GROUP

*For Caroline*
*and*
*all the other storytellers to come*

# Contents

PART III

## *Otheren*

# Acknowledgments

My undying gratitude and love go to my family—Howell and Debbie Graham, Molly and Russ Allred, and my favorite grandchild, Caroline Allred—a tireless cheerleading team and tolerant subjects for so many commentaries. But most especially, I thank my husband, Ernie, who makes me laugh and always believes in me.

Thank you, dear old friends (and I mean that in every sense of each of those words): Knox Pierson, Jane Grant, Maggie Aardema, and Nancy Millen, my buddies who never hesitate to let fly with opinions (especially Knox, proofreader *extraordinaire*). For their encouragement, I thank my writer pal and Southern sistah, Celia Rivenbark, and my writers' group: Wanda Canada, Jean Nance, Richard Triebe, Ellen Rickert, Kay Schaal, and John Nunheh. Without Tami Mansur, computer genius and friend to PC illiterates, my computer woes would be overwhelming . . . many thanks. Thanks also go to Maury Tepper, so generous with his expertise; to Ben Steelman, who keeps me in the loop; and to Sarah Bird Wright, in gratitude for her advice and her good sense in all matters of writing. And I confess a continuing admiration for Pat Conroy, ever the Southern gentleman.

I offer heartfelt thanks for the generosity and great kindness of Dr. Richard Holland and his wife, Becky; to the folks at the University of West Alabama; and to all the ever-hospitable citizens of Livingston, my favorite small town.

I must also acknowledge Michelle Zumbro, the everlasting optimist who helps "make memories" (even if the expression does make me gag); Lucy Parlange, who always kept the faith; Mandy Johnson, whose beautiful cover brings a Southern smile; Scott Simpson, supreme WHQR Public Radio producer, who makes me sound better than I really do, and whose ear is always right on the money; and the WHQR staff and our listeners, who have been so faithful and supportive, and whose loyalty I appreciate more than I can say.

And finally, my thanks go to the folks at John F. Blair, Publisher, for their willingness to make this happen, among them Steve Kirk, my editor, and especially Carolyn Sakowski.

# Introduction

This all began in 1995, so you can see I haven't been at it that long. The writing, I mean. That January, my first commentary for WHQR Public Radio was aired, a four-minute piece on the changes in the small town of Livingston, Alabama, since my childhood summers there. The little county seat had become gentrified in the past decade or so, and the essay was a quirky then-and-now piece. The station liked it, and so did the listeners. "They like me!" I felt like an elderly Sally Field. (Well, maybe not elderly. Sally is no spring chicken.) I became the new Southern voice for the station.

A major change born of this late-blooming career is that I have become a bottom feeder. Having to write a radio commentary every other Thursday, the pressure is on. I am always on the lookout for loony stories, nutty characters, and unique aspects of Southern life. Actually, I discovered that what we consider our Southern world is quite universal.

One woman at a book signing said, "I love your stories about small-town life. It's exactly like the place where I grew up."

"What part of Alabama are you from?" I asked.

"Oh, I'm from New Hampshire."

Gertrude Stein was right: A small town is a small town is a small town.

During the first five years, I wrote enough essays to publish in a book, *Turn South at the Next Magnolia . . . Directions from a Lifelong Southerner*. This new book reflects my continuing observations of the South, small towns, fruitcakes I have known, and card-carrying eccentrics. (If you have a sister with a bunny named Rabbit E. Lee, your family qualifies as Southern!) The particular focus is on the characters who populate this changing world. I have designated them *Southeren* (for the natives), *Brotheren* (for both blood relations and kindred spirits), and *Otheren* (for those resisting pigeonholes).

Who should read this book? All Southerners and everybody who has ever known a Southerner or is curious about the breed. I consider it an essential field guide for all the newcomers to our South. It will give you a real sense of who and what we are.

The title *In a Magnolia Minute* and the subtitle *Secrets of a Late Bloomer* suggest a strong sense of time. According to writer Brendan Gill, the sculptor Louise Nevelson first exhibited and sold her work when she was in her fifties, Edith Hamilton wrote *The Greek Way* at sixty-three, Grandma Moses took up painting in her seventies, and Brooke Astor wrote her first novel in her eighties . . . so there are worlds out there to be conquered at any age. The word on the street is that fifty is the new thirty, and I'm making book on that!

Take some time to meet my friends and have a good laugh. Maybe, just maybe, you will be inspired to take a minute (magnolia or not) to capture some of the priceless pieces of your own life.

# Part I
## Southeren

# Extra Credit

I tear them from magazines, clip them from newspapers, and copy them from books and letters. I'm addicted. I collect quotations.

Some quotes tweak my imagination, delight me with a striking image, or reveal insight that never occurred to me. Sometimes, it is the precision of the words that pleases.

Unlike Forrest Gump's box of chocolates, in which you never know what you're going to get, my collection of quotes is more a Whitman's Sampler. You know, the one with the seating chart for every piece of candy: pecan nougat: third from the left, second row. My quotes fall loosely under the following categories: humor, inspiration, and mind expansion.

For humor, H. L. Mencken: "A cynic is a man who, when he smells flowers, looks around for a coffin."

Or Mrs. Astor's classic remark as she was herded into a lifeboat that dark April night aboard the *Titanic*: "I rang for ice, but this is ridiculous."

For inspiration: "There are two ways to live your life. One is

as though nothing is a miracle. The other is as though everything is a miracle." Einstein

"We make a living by what we get. We make a life by what
we give." Anonymous

For mind expansion: "Trust in God, but tie your camel."
Arabian proverb

"There are only the pursued and the pursuing, the busy and
the tired." F. Scott Fitzgerald, *The Great Gatsby*.

My fascination with these bons mots began, strangely
enough, in tenth-grade plane geometry class. My family's genetic flaw surfaces every generation with Mendelian regularity:
the absence of a left brain. Its cranial space is filled by an overdeveloped right brain. Translation: We are severely challenged
mathematically.

I always fail to understand word problems: If A digs half as
fast as B, who digs 4¾ feet every 15.6 minutes, why does C always win the competition? It is akin to pondering eternity.

When I was in high school, my counselor assured me that
plane geometry was different from other math. It was spatial,
like drawing, and I would find it more amenable than algebra. I
soon discovered that I had been cruelly deceived.

But Miss Ruby Gulley, our geometry teacher at Tuscaloosa
High, was a kind and patient soul. I thought this gray-haired
woman in rimless glasses was ancient, but in those days before
Jane Fonda and Cher, she was probably in her forties and only
seemed to us to be Mrs. Haversham from *Great Expectations*.

The geometry room had a large placard over the top of the
triple blackboard. The quotation went something like this:

"The measure of a man's real character is what he
would do if he knew he would never be found out."
Thomas Babington McCauley (1800-1859)

It appeared to be an admonition to potential cheaters, but
the implications on a wider scale led me to contemplate a moral

landscape. I copied the quotation on the cover of my Blue Horse spiral notebook and traced over the words through the semester whenever my mind wandered. McCauley's quote became a heady tidbit for my sophomoric mind, and was certainly more engaging to contemplate than the sides of an isosceles triangle.

At the end of the year, we entered Miss Gulley's final exam with sweaty palms. Or at least I did. Hunching over the problems, I worked feverishly.

At the end of the exam was a large star. "Bonus problem," it said. "Ten points. Write out the quotation by Thomas Babington McCauley. Recall any ideas or thoughts you may have had on its meaning."

I looked up. The quotation placard had been removed from its spot over the blackboard. I began to write.

Miss Gulley understood that a cautionary maxim for cheaters could also be a feast for dreamers. Best of all, she knew that ten extra-credit points were pure gold to all of us students missing a left brain.

# Aye, There's the Rub

I take my seat in the doctor's office, pick up a 1999 copy of *Time* magazine, and sit next to an elderly man and his wife. The man, in a heavily starched white shirt and creased jeans, is in mid-conversation. The waiting room is mesmerized by the recitation. He holds court amongst the eight of us as if he were Elmer Gantry preaching to the masses. He is a spellbinder. Our magazines lie in our laps or remain poised in midair, unread, pages unturned.

"Yessir," he says, "been using Vicks VapoRub for eighty-three years now. Use it for every little hurt I get, and inside of twenty-four hours, there ain't a bruise mark left." He points to his unbruised forearm.

"Rub it on my knees and elbows ever day, and the arthur ritis disappears." He moves his feet and arms as if he were lifting weights.

This reminds me of one of Mama's favorite jokes.

One woman to another: "How you doing?"

"Well, I ain't been doing too good. Been in bed with arthur ritis."

Other women, giggling: "Oh mercy, ain't them Ritis brothers somethin'!"

The elderly man continues, "Eat a tablespoonful first thing in the morning, and my innards is lubricated just right, and I don't have no plumbing trouble a-tall.

"Put a dab on my ingrown toenail, and it grows right in no time. Toenail fungus . . . gone." He holds out a foot for our inspection, but the effect is lost, since it is shod in a large black Nike.

"See any wrinkles on this face?" I peer into his smooth face. "Rub Vicks on my face ever night since I was a pup. Nary a wrinkle.

"See this here?"

We all lean forward. He pulls his collar aside to reveal his octogenarian neck.

"Had that Roto-Rooter operation on my karate artery and rubbed Vicks into the scar afterwards and poof . . . gone. Had a triple bypass six years ago and looky here."

He pulls the neck of his shirt open to reveal a faint scar on his chest.

"Rubbed it in four days after the operation and bingo . . . no scar."

He goes on to tell us that the ever-versatile salve can be rubbed on the pole of a bird feeder to repel squirrels, that it can be used as an acne cure, and that it is even applied by animal trainers on bear cubs when they are returned to their mothers to dispel the scent of humans.

And what is this New Age miracle medicine, this duct tape of the patent-medicine world? North Carolina's own Vicks VapoRub, an original Tar Heel product like Pepsi Cola, developed in 1905 by H. S. Richardson in Selma, North Carolina, down the road from Ava Gardner's Smithfield.

Vicks' innovative remedy of menthol, camphor, and petroleum jelly was originally sold under the catchy name of Richardson's Croup and Pneumonia Cure Salve. Apparently, pneumonia set in before you could even tell the druggist what you wanted, the name was so long. The name was changed to Magic Croup Salve. Then Vicks Salve appeared on the label, and eventually the alliterative Vicks VapoRub. The great flu epidemic of 1918 made Vicks the most popular treatment of the time and assured its success.

Our man in the waiting room continues holding forth on other remedies. My favorite is his solution for the infant problem of mouth thrush, although the cure does not involve the magic of Vicks.

To cure infant thrush, he pronounces, find a person who had never seen his daddy. You might even have to go to another county to find him, but once the fatherless person is located, he must hold the afflicted infant and breathe three times into its little mouth. As soon as this is done, the thrush fungus will disappear.

The old man looks around at us, casing his audience, checking our reaction to this latest bit. But the spell is broken. Though we were enthralled by the Vicks saga, Elmer Gantry's thrush cure proves too much even for us. We return to our dog-eared magazines and continue our endless wait in silence.

# Phat Chance

In this age of the size-four dress (a recent invention . . . I can remember when a size ten was considered tiny), talk of diets and weight is constant. None of us is actually on a diet, of course. We call them "programs," as if somehow that will take the sting out of our nine-hundred-calorie day.

I think the previous generation had a kinder and more humane view of what constituted a figure of gracious plenty—"an abundance," as Aunt Julia used to say, or a woman with what Mama called a "D.A.R. bosom."

That was the golden age of euphemisms. I never recall anyone being called "fat." It simply wasn't done, any more than you would call someone "ugly." You might call them "unfortunate," yes; "homely," maybe; but "ugly," . . . never.

We said a fat woman was "big boned" or "stout," a favorite adjective you rarely hear nowadays. For a man, it was different. He was "portly" or "heavy-set," kindly terms still used today for any male resembling Moby-Dick. It's a tougher world for women.

When someone did manage to lose weight, we said he or

she had "fallen off," a Southern euphemism for "dropped a ton." "Cud'n Clarisse sure has fallen off since I saw her last Christmas," we'd say. I never understood what the person had fallen off of, unless it was a mountain of banana pudding or a four-foot wedge of pecan pie.

I still remember when we lived in Charleston and went to a Spoleto Festival performance of *Tosca* featuring a well-endowed diva clad in brocade. The Charleston newspaper reviewer called her "a singing upholstered sofa," a cruel comment for a stellar musical performance. But image is all.

In college, I gained the freshman fifteen and then some and was a bit ample myself. To top it off, I hennaed my hair and dyed my eyebrows and eyelashes black, a prehistoric attempt at punk back when we called punks "J.D.'s"—juvenile delinquents. My rebellion was brief. When Daddy came to pick me up for summer break, he took one look at me and said, "My God, you look just like Belle Watling!" the famed madam in *Gone with the Wind*. He refused to take me home until I washed the henna out of my hair, but there was no quick fix for the rest of my makeover. The brows, lashes, and weight were to be a summer project.

When we stopped off at Grandmama's house for lunch on the way home, her cook, Betty, took one gander at the freshman fifteen and informed me that I looked "mighty pretty and mighty prosperous." I consider that the most diplomatic and generous remark I've ever heard. Betty missed her calling. She should have been the ambassador to France.

I did "fall off" before September. After all, I was transferring to Chapel Hill and had to be at my fighting trim to enter that commie, pinko, liberal school, as the Alabama cousins called it.

My daughter tells me that "phat" is now the new compliment. "Man, she is phat"—meaning hot, fabulous, terrific. But if you say someone is "phat," how do you know how it's spelled?

Will I use this new expression and say to my friends, "Hey, you're looking phat today"? Fat chance!

# By Any Other Name

We are all affected by the sounds, meanings, and implications of the personal names—both fictional and real—that we hear. The comic strip "Kudzu" certainly uses names to full advantage. The Southern belle cheerleader is named Veranda. The hypocritical preacher is Will B. Dunn . . . perfect. In the nineteenth century, Dickens tagged his characters with names reflecting their dispositions, virtues, and vices. The villainous Murdstones, sniveling Uriah Heep, and skinflint Ebenezer Scrooge are all familiar names custom-cut visually and phonetically by the author to reflect the essence of his memorable characters.

Sometimes in real life, we don't even notice the wacky name combinations we encounter. My mama had a highly developed sense of humor and a keen ear for the absurd. She loved to tell about the infamous Hogg sisters from Texas, Ima and Ura. But she failed to see anything unusual or humorous about the name of her next-door neighbor, Miss Olive Branch.

My daddy's favorite name joke was this old chestnut. A man comes into court to request to legally change his name.

Judge says, "What is your name, sir?"

The man says, "George Stinkovitch."

Judge, suppressing a smile: "I certainly can see why you want to change your name. What would you like to change it to?"

The man says, "Harry Stinkovitch, Your Honor."

The origins of names are fun, especially surnames. Surnames may reflect a variety of occupations. Some are obvious: Fisher, Baker, Butler. Their origins are immediately recognizable and clear. But other familiar occupation names like Fletcher, Turner, and Cooper are less easily understood. Their beginnings are obscured by the fact that their occupations no longer exist in our machine age. Fletcher means "arrow maker," an important munitions manufacturer in the Middle Ages. Turners were those skilled carpenters who turned or worked lathes long before the Industrial Age of machine-made furniture. The cooper, or barrel maker, was an essential craftsman whose wares held everything from pickles to fine wines in the days before mass-produced glass containers.

First names are an entirely different matter, since they are chosen, rather than assumed like surnames. Babies have long been named for bygone or living relatives, especially in the South. But this seems to be a declining trend in most parts of the country. First names of cities and states are now in vogue. Dakota, Dallas, Madison, Austin, Savannah, and, of course, Paris are becoming chichi in some circles. I have high hopes that Peoria, Opelika, Fuquay-Varina, and Biloxi will be added to the list.

A surprising trend is toward choosing biblical names. An abundance of Sarahs, Jonathans, Davids, Jacobs, and Joshuas are showing up, edging out Tiffanys and Brandons. Eve and Leah also make the charts these days. Even Oprah is a biblical name gone wrong—a misspelling of the Old Testament name Orpha, we're told.

Some names are linked to historic events or people at the center of those events. My own son was born on February 20, the historic day astronaut John Glenn orbited the earth and the nation was riveted to the television. I remember it well. The nursing staff was so glued to the TV that I could have birthed a marmoset and no one would have batted an eye.

My husband, being a captain in the Marine Corps at the time, wanted to name our son for this groundbreaking Marine hero. I demurred, somewhat vigorously. Hundreds of other mothers did not. *Life* magazine the next week came out with a feature article on the hundreds of John Glenns born on February 20—John Glenn Stevenson, John Glenn Vanetti, John Glenn LaSalle, John Glenn Epstein, and so forth.

But the prize name and its tiny recipient were featured on the cover of *Life* that week. The close-up of Mr. and Mrs. Hill's newborn son was adorable. Today, some forty-odd years later, there is a man out there who knows all too well how names can result from historic moments and haunt the recipients for the rest of their lives. At large, Orbit Hill, a living testimony to his parents' whimsical and bizarre choice.

# Adam's House Cat

"I'M MERT," the license plate on the Bronco ahead of me reads. I drive behind it for blocks, wondering who Mert is and why he or she wants this vehicular introduction. Gender is obscured, but maybe that is intentional. "I'M MERT." I'm Merton? I'm Merwin? I'm Myrtle? I'm Mertroyd?

The windows are tinted, so I can't get a view of the car's occupant. However, as I drive through traffic on Market Street, "I'M MERT" does make me think of those names of unknown folk we use all the time, names free-floating in the ether.

For instance, "I don't know him from Adam." Dickens used the expression in *The Old Curiosity Shop* back in 1840. "He called to see my Governor this morning . . . and beyond that, I don't know him from Adam," the great storyteller wrote.

Of course, we do know who Adam was, but he hardly had an extensive network of buddies. Who would have known him, much less his personal menagerie? So if I don't know Adam, I certainly do not know his cat, as in "I don't know him from Adam's house cat." It's nice to think that Adam *had* a house cat to rub against his bare legs on those chilly forty-degree mornings when he was cursing his skimpy fig leaf and snarling at Eve that it was her fault they were no longer in the comfy hothouse luxury of Eden.

Notice we don't say, "I don't know him from Adam's Chihuahua," though we do say, "Adam's off-ox," a particular favorite of mine. If we don't know him from Adam's off-ox, do we know him from Adam's on-ox? It must all boil down to the fact that it was such a long time ago nobody alive would remember Adam or his pets. But that does seem to state the obvious.

And what about Eve's menagerie? Why not "I don't know her from Eve's hamster" or "I don't know her from Eve's parakeet"? It's chauvinistic, to say the least, though Monsieur Chauvin would not give a name to this kind of discrimination until several millennia had passed.

A favorite of Mama's was also biblical. "Why, he is as poor as Job's turkey," she'd say. Now, Job had his problems, God knows. But was his turkey more poverty stricken than his neighbors' poultry or our own Carolina gobblers? The thinking might have been that not only was Job a pitiful pauper but that, by extension, his turkey was doubly cursed to have such an insolvent owner.

"Hobson's choice" showed up as early at 1617, from the obstinate Tobias Hobson, a stable owner in Cambridge, England, who insisted that the rider take the horse for hire nearest the door, rather than the horse of the customer's choosing. So, having Hobson's choice now means no choice at all. It is a term frequently bandied about during election years.

And Morpheus. We take the poetic phrase "in the arms of Morpheus" to mean sleeping, but that is not quite true. Morpheus was the god of dreams, not sleep. It was his father, Hypnos, who was the god of sleep. Poor Hypnos gets no press at all. It's another misuse of a name, but I'm sure the gods don't lose much shut eye over the error.

And what about "every Tom, Dick, and Harry"? Who were

they? Generic beings, apparently. Tom, Dick, and Harry were popular names 250-odd years ago when the phrase appeared in the *Vocal Miscellany*. The Tom, Dick, and Harry roster does not hold true for the twenty-first century. Today, it should be "every Michael, Keith, and Ethan."

Okay, "I'M MERT" is going straight onto Water Street, and I've got to turn here onto Front Street, right behind that gray Volvo with a license plate that says, "HENPECKED." I wonder who would admit to that description in this day of the threatened male ego. Maybe if I speed up a bit, I can see . . .

# Mississippi Mishap

Amidst threats of hurricanes, terrorist alerts, and political jockeying for the upcoming election of 2004, eighty-six-year-old Mike Wallace was handcuffed and arrested by Taxi and Limousine Commission officers who apparently trained at the Taliban School of Etiquette. His offense: Wallace asked, "What is the problem?" when the officers approached his limo driver double-parked outside a Manhattan restaurant where Mike had run in to pick up a takeout order of meat loaf. He apparently repeated the scurrilous question several times. I've never been a Mike Wallace fan, but I am going to write him a sympathy letter. I feel his pain.

Think a hundred-plus-degree heat in the early afternoon. The little Mississippi town lay baking in the July sun, a handful of cars cruising lethargically around the town square. It was a perfect afternoon for heat stroke . . . or antiquing. At least that's what my daughter and I thought. Little did we know we were headed for our own Southern-fried Mike Wallace moment.

We moseyed around the square but saw no antique shops. I

pulled over at the P.O. and asked a lady going in if there was an antique store anywhere in town.

"Why, sure," she said. "You just passed one yonder across the street. Just turn around and go back half a block. It's on the other side next to Tree Frog Gifts."

I thanked her and proceeded to do just what she suggested. As we pulled into a parking place and got out of the car, I noticed a blue light reflecting in my window. A short female officer in a skin-tight police uniform was right behind me.

"License," she said.

I handed it over and said, "Am I in a no-parking zone?"

The sausage was walking back to her car. I could hear her radioing in my North Carolina license plate. I wondered if she thought the Honda was stolen. Surely not. I was not in my chop-shop outfit but rather in my aging Southern matron ensemble.

"What did I do?" I asked, walking toward the police car.

"Back to your vehicle," Officer Angry hissed. I wondered why she was so furious.

We waited in the broiling sun.

She returned, handed me a ticket, and said, "I am confiscating your driver's license."

"What did I do? How can I drive?"

"Illegal U-turn. Just show them this ticket if you get stopped. Your court date is the twenty-eighth of next month. Any questions, go to city hall." Officer Angry stormed back to the police car. Her fury was as palpable as my dismay.

"Can we talk about this?" I whimpered to her retreating back. The black-and-white burned rubber leaving the scene of the crime.

We walked to the tiny city hall. Police Chief Thomas was not available at the moment. He was at the junior high school, they said, tending to a snake with a yen for education, but he would be back shortly.

Eventually, a tall Morgan Freeman look-alike arrived. I gave a plaintive explanatory rehash of the day's events. Morgan shook his head. We were on our way, driver's license in hand, exchanged for my ticket by the kindly Morgan Freeman.

The moral of the story? Take your pick:

Watch where you U-turn

Police power can be frightening

Civility is on the wane

Barney Fife has had a sex change operation, gained a few pounds, and moved to Mississippi, where she is alive and well

# Sidekick: Travels with Eleanor Roosevelt

In the summer of 2002, my roommate Betsy from Chapel Hill days joined me for another trip through the Delta country. Our Elvis/Faulkner trip through Mississippi and Tennessee several years ago had been such a success that we thought we would give the Deep South another whirl. The Delta is foreign territory for East Coast Betsy, who grew up in Durham and got her master's at Yale after UNC, whereas I am like Brer Rabbit back in the briar patch, savoring every minute in the thicket of the Deep South.

Betsy emerges from her cultural cocoon for these trips. How can a woman who counsels "to-be-weds" at Arlington Chapel next to the cemetery (who knew folks could be married as well as buried at Arlington?), raised three sons to adulthood, and lives in the hip environs of D.C. lead such a sheltered life? Traveling with Betsy is like touring with an alien.

Betsy is the only sixty-something person I know who has never heard of *American Idol*, *SpongeBob SquarePants*, Brad Pitt, or body piercing and hasn't seen a single movie since *Risky*

*Business*. She is blissfully unaware that Liberace has been dead for nearly two decades and that reflexology has nothing to do with Tourette's syndrome. An innocent abroad in pop culture, Betsy doesn't subscribe to cable TV or own a cell phone, a VCR, a hot comb, or a garage door opener. Her mother lived to ninety-five, so she has a long and clueless life ahead. She is the ultimate Luddite and a great traveling companion. Who else would be impressed by the Wendy's drive-through? To think you can get fast food through a window is miraculous to my friend! And imagine, senior discounts are out there for the taking, if you only know to ask.

A pragmatist, when her dentist recommended a mouthpiece to prevent nocturnal teeth grinding, Betsy deemed the cost excessive. She went to a sports equipment store and bought a regulation soccer mouthpiece, which works perfectly well, thank you very much. The only drawback is the bizarre appearance it gives to the sleeper. The mouth guard transforms my sleeping friend into first runner-up in the Eleanor Roosevelt Look-Alike Contest. I feel as if we should be accompanied by the Secret Service.

Our last night in Memphis, after watching the Flying Elvi, sixteen in all, parachute from a plane and perform with cardboard guitars in Handy Square on Beale Street, we headed back to the car. Betsy was the designated night driver, since riding with me after dark is like being piloted by a human mole. I have turned into a Sunshine Girl in my old age. I drive only in daylight.

Betsy wanted one last look at the mighty Mississippi, so we swung down to the waterfront. Memphis is not known as a safe city even among natives, and we had been cautioned about the waterfront area. We locked the doors. As we headed north, we missed the turn that would have led us out of the area. We were disgorged onto the elevated expressway . . . and were promptly lost.

"I'll just pop down and see where we are," Betsy said.

I looked at my watch. It was well after midnight. We descended to the seedy streets beneath the off-ramp, and the opening scene of *The Bonfire of the Vanities* danced in my brain. Few people were out except for knots of young men moving in surly groups along the dark street. Betsy slowed for a stop sign.

"Don't stop," I hissed. "Just roll on through. Keep moving. Don't stop."

We cruised through the projects, two old ladies in a rented car, one crouched almost on the floor, riding shotgun. At last, we saw a ramp to take us out of the underbelly of Memphis and back to the lighted road of Taco Bells and Krispy Kremes. I had never realized how beautiful neon is.

As we unlocked our motel room, I looked at Betsy numbly.

"Honestly, now, weren't you the least bit afraid back there?" I asked.

"Oh, yeah," she nodded, reaching for her Eleanor Roosevelt soccer apparatus. "I was afraid, all right. I was afraid you were going to kill me."

# Directions from a Lifelong Southerner

In the War Between the States, the Union army named battle-grounds for bodies of water, while the Confederates named them for landmarks. The Battle of Bull Run at Bull Run Creek was known to Confederates as the Battle of Manassas, for Manassas Junction. For Union supporters, it was the Battle of Antietam. For Confederates, it was the Battle of Sharpsburg. And so on. This disparity in description is alive and well today, even among Southern families. It all depends on the genes.

State historical road markers in the South always mark an incorrect spot, observed my transplant friend, Nicki. The birth-place of Whistler's mother or the home of Mary Baker Eddy is usually two blocks north of the sign or a third of a mile west of the marker in the South. Nicki claims that in all other parts of the country, historical markers are placed on the actual spot, not four blocks south. Alexander Hamilton's residence was here, the sign will say, not a quarter-mile south of the marker. It's a bit obsessive-compulsive, in my book.

I married into a large Southern family who speak in numbers.

I realized this early on. It is especially noticeable in the initial exchange of greetings whenever the clan gets together. The first fifteen minutes of conversation after anyone arrives at a family gathering are fully focused on how the arrivee arrived. The opening shot is always, "Hey, how did y'all come this time?"

"We took Highway 95 to the 344 exit," they will say, "and then turned west onto Service Road 2961."

"Oh," one of the siblings or cousins will reply. "Didn't you come on 281 to Benson the last time, then take I-40 West?"

My reaction to this opening number, excuse the pun, is as volatile today as ever. I have to check myself to keep from becoming surly. "Who cares how you came?" I want to snap. "You're here. Can we now have a conversation that does not involve a number in any way, shape, or form?"

But their highway litany continues, meandering through the interstates and back roads of North Carolina and the surrounding states. The recitation of road numbers must play itself out. It is a genetic collective unconscious pattern worthy of Jung.

I married into a family with overdeveloped left brains stuffed with numbers and mathematical formulae. But I come from a long line of DNA that assures us of no discernible left-brain function at all. My family never knows which highway or road we're on unless it has a proper name. The old Blue and Gray highway. The highway to New Orleans. The Rooster Bridge. We rarely talk about it. We find it a minor miracle that we manage to get from point A to point B at all and are loath to discuss embarrassing details like wrong roads taken. Routes are never a topic of conversation.

I've never met a highway number I really liked. I have managed to store and retrieve I-40 and I-95, but that's about it. The old metes-and-bounds approach to directions is inbred in my family. You know how that works. Going to the place that sells local honey or Silver Queen corn? Okay. Ride to the stoplight past the Owl Motel to the corner where there's an Exxon sign, turn left in front of it, and go 'til you get to the new Krispy Kreme.

You'll pass Folsom's Used Cars on the right. It's not too many blocks now. If you pass the Piggly Wiggly, you've gone too far. You'll have to backtrack. Okay, slow down after the Krispy Kreme because you'll be coming up on a dirt road to your left pretty soon and a barbwire fence in front of a doublewide with a yellow door. Turn there. Go on down a little bit 'til you get to the big oak tree on the right side just in front of a "See Rock City" sign painted on the barn roof. Keep on just past the creek bridge and you'll see the Silver Queen man's house from there. It's a red-brick split-level with a Toyota on cinder blocks in the front yard and painted tires lining the walk.

Now, those are what I call directions. Please note that there is not a single number in the entire directive.

Our big Borden family reunion at a country farm near Pittsboro is coming up soon. It's almost a three-hour drive. The question is, should we go on I-40 to 64 and take the 342 exit . . . or just head for the Triangle and pray we get there before the barbecue and hush puppies give out?

# High on the Hog

First, the technical stuff. What *is* the difference between a pig and a hog? It's a weight thing. At 120 pounds, a pig graduates to a hog. The word *hog* is both a noun and a verb. One can be it or do it.

Idioms involving pigs and hogs are many and varied but often suggest our misguided perceptions of the nature of the beast. We say that we "pig out" or "eat like a pig," yet the pig, unlike the horse, knows when it has had enough. A horse will eat until it dies of its own excess. You cannot "sweat like a pig" because pigs do not even have sweat glands. This accounts for those long, luxurious wallows in the cool mud.

We say we may have to "hogtie" someone to get them to do something. Those someones are usually husbands, some of whom may be "male chauvinist pigs." Our closet can become a "pigpen" or our teenager's bedroom a virtual "pigsty."

If a thing is absurd, we call it "hogwash." When something is not very likely (winning the lottery?), we say it will occur "in a pig's eye" or "when pigs fly." We are cautioned against buying "a pig in a poke." Some of us try desperately to "make a silk purse out of a sow's ear." We've all heard our children lament, "But he's hogging the TV!"

We all go "hog wild" from time to time and "live high on the hog." But to do that, we need to "bring home the bacon." If you steal the spotlight, you're a real "ham." If someone's behavior is truly unacceptable, he is a "swine."

If we are deliriously happy and things are going splendidly, we're in "hog heaven." Biblically speaking, we all know the futility of "tossing pearls before swine," a concept that flashes across every schoolteacher's mind in pensive moments.

Yet a five-year British research project has revealed the pig to have the highest intelligence of any barnyard animal. Pigs are easily housebroken and can be taught to retrieve, race competitively, dance, pull carts, and sniff out land mines. This is more than can be said for many spouses.

My personal acquaintance with real hogs has been limited to an enormous Berkshire named Bacon, a resident of the working farm at Middleton Plantation in Charleston that could barely upright himself when you approached. I'm more familiar with the pigs in literature, rhymes, and stories, beginning with "This little piggy went to market" and the cautionary tale of "The Three Little Pigs." My granddaughter's favorite books in her youngest days were *The Pig and the Pancake* and *Olivia*. Other classic snout-nosed heroes are Wilbur in *Charlotte's Web*, the baby—alias the pig—in *Alice in Wonderland*, Beatrix Potter's Pigling Bland, and the ever-fearful Piglet in *Winnie the Pooh*. For adults, there's Napoleon in Orwell's political satire *Animal Farm*. Porky Pig still stutters and salivates on the small screen on Saturday mornings. The Muppets hottie is the irrepressible Miss Piggy. The film *Babe* elevated the pig to Oscar status, an innocent in a world of guile and deceit. The innocent was sent abroad in the sequel, *Babe: Pig in the City*.

A more useful animal would be hard to find. For your dinner table: hams, porkchops, cracklings, bacon, barbecue, chitlins.

On New Year's Eve, Southerners enjoy those lucky hog jowls with black-eyed peas and collards, which ensures plenty of good fortune and greenbacks for the coming year. There is pigskin for your shoes, your belt, your pocketbook, and, of course, your football. Pigs provide bristles for brushes, the source for insulin, and heart valves for cardiac patients. For epicureans, they unearth truffles. What other animal does quite so much for man and remains a creature of great good humor . . . and the target of ridicule?

Hogs are in the news on a daily basis: hog lagoons, conglomerate hog-farm mergers, and hog-waste spills, all of which seem to involve our tax dollars. But all in all, hogs and pigs are intelligent, useful, sensible creatures. Now, if we could only say as much about the human beings who rule their collective existence—those politicians and pig farmers. Think about it the next time you cruise I-40 with your windows rolled down.

# Dreamland: A Religious Experience

Everybody talks about how hard this place is to find—this Jerusalem Heights, where the famous Dreamland Barbeque is located. Go down McFarland Avenue, which slices through the town of Tuscaloosa and the University of Alabama, and turn left on Jug Factory Road. You'll wind among kudzu-covered telephone poles and rusted-out truck carcasses in the process of being swallowed whole by the ubiquitous vine. The kudzu is lush in the summer sun. Recent rains have washed the red dust from the leaves, each larger than your two hands. The tendrils creep over and cover every object in their path.

Keep driving past the Almega Casket Company on your right (you'll wonder briefly if this is an omen) and continue up the hill. As your car adjusts to the rise and passes "Miles and Smiles" Auto Repair and New Life Baptist Church, you'll wonder if the casket company and the church are some sort of signs as you ascend to Jerusalem Heights. The trip to barbecue heaven has taken a definite ecclesiastical turn. Dreamland signs, paint peeling, peep through the kudzu to reassure the pilgrim that he is on the right track . . . as does the steady stream of cars crawling upward toward the heavenly barbecue shack, chimney rising out of the middle of the roof, heavy plume of smoke drifting heavenward in the still August heat. It is midday and the sun beats mercilessly against the tin roof. Several saggy hound dogs lope forlornly around to the back of the small frame building as my car pulls in.

The founder of this mythic eating establishment was Big Daddy Bishop, who has gone to his reward from his labors on Jerusalem Heights. But he is not really gone. Big Daddy's smiling image, pipe in teeth, is everywhere—on Styrofoam cups, on the wax-paper insert in the basket under your ribs, on the sauce label, on the T-shirts and hats. Big Daddy looks like a cross between George Foreman and Popeye.

I check out the interior décor, which gives the word *eclectic* new meaning. Christmas lights snake along the walls; big dice cubes serve as drinking-straw holders at the bar; license plates are nailed to walls and ceiling. Competing with Big Daddy's image is that of a smiling Bear Bryant—patron saint of Alabama—papering the walls. Bear came to coach the Crimson Tide the same year that Dreamland opened, 1958. Both the Crimson Tide icon and Dreamland are legendary in these parts.

A large sign above the bar reads, "And on the 8th day, well, you know . . ." The biblical theme persists, permeating the place. You realize barbecue is a religious experience here, much as it is in North Carolina.

The place is packed. I sidle up to the bar and check the posted lunch items above yet another Bear Bryant portrait. A traveling salesman working out of Rocky Mount, North Carolina, tells me about Ray Perkins, who played for the Bear. The salesman, elbow deep in red sauce dripping from his pork ribs, which he attacks like corn on the cob, goes off on a tangent about a boy from North Carolina who played for the Crimson Tide in the sixties and never returned to the Carolinas. He stayed and became a radio sports commentator. I must look like a Crimson

Tide supporter because he drones on and on about this player as if I'm supposed to know him, pausing only briefly in his homily to lick his fingers and grab a paper towel from the upright holder on the bar.

I study the menu, monastic in its simplicity:

BBQ rib sandwich . . . $5.25    3 ribs and 4 slices of Sunbeam

BBQ plate . . . $8.95    6 ribs and 6 slices of white bread and a cup of trademark dipping sauce

BBQ slab . . . $16.95    12 ribs (This hungry-man portion is for to-go orders. For all I know, it may come with a whole loaf of Sunbeam as a "side.")

Not a green vegetable in sight.

I order the rib sandwich, which arrives promptly with its tidy stack of white bread and a Co-Cola (the correct pronunciation in these parts). Having no clue how to attack the dripping ribs as a sandwich or what to do with the bread, I pick up the ribs corn-on-the-cob-style like my salesman buddy and end up using the bread as a Sunbeam sponge to mop up Big Daddy's barbecue sauce, which rolls in uncontrolled rivulets down my arms.

Big Daddy's motto—"Ain't NOTHING like 'em"—doesn't begin to cover the experience. The ribs are very good. I could do without the white bread. And the atmosphere? It is everything I could have dreamed of.

# Taking Care of Bidness

The innovative business spirit has always been an American trait, but some Horatio Algers may have gone too far. In a bizarre entrepreneurial event, the house on Second Street opened up as a bed-and-breakfast some years ago, with emphasis on catering to honeymoon couples. This B&B in Fall River, Massachusetts, is the modest railroad flat house where Lizzie Borden and her unfortunate parents lived, until that August day in 1892 left Lizzie and her sister orphans in the badly stained two-story Victorian horror chamber. Apparently, the Lizzie Borden Bed & Breakfast does a brisk business, especially around the August 4 anniversary and at Halloween. The ghoulish double murder, rather than discouraging customers, seems to be precisely the point. The old jump-rope rhyme

Lizzie Borden took an ax,
Gave her mother forty whacks,
When she saw what she had done,
She gave her father forty-one

isn't exactly *Lohengrin* but must be music to some newlyweds' ears.

Southerners are just as enterprising as their New England neighbors. You can now rent shacks on Mississippi plantations, remnants of long-gone days. The quarters have been updated with electricity and running water, so the vacationers don't get full-monty poverty. The upgrades soften the historical impact of living down the road from the big house. The plantation owners have found this a lucrative business. Guests generally have three or four shacks to choose from. The quarters all have names: the Robert Johnson Shack, the W. C. Handy Place, and so on. Blues-music lovers and unsuspecting Yankees flock to these Delta experiences, while owners count more than Confederate dollars.

"Bidness," as Tennessee Williams called it, has taken another strange turn down South. Death and food go hand in hand in these parts, as anyone attending a funeral can tell you. Southerners celebrate with food and console with food. Wedding: Bring on the shrimp and red velvet cake. Baby shower: Roll out the finger sandwiches and deviled eggs. Funeral: Haul out the casseroles and the barbecue.

One Georgia entrepreneur, according to Cox News Service, cashed in on this connection with an interesting combo business. Frank Price petitioned the city council of Summerville, Georgia, to allow him to open a crematory next door to his barbecue stand. He plans to buy secondhand equipment from the notorious Tri-State Crematory in Noble, Georgia, whose careless owners misplaced clients' bodies and are presently enjoying bread and water in the prison system of a state that understands these things. A stream south of Atlanta isn't called Hard Labor Creek for nothing.

The ambitious Mr. Price is accustomed to the concept of piggybacking businesses, if you'll pardon the expression. His funeral home used to be next door to his previous business: The Barbecue Barn. It might be said that Price espouses a cause-and-effect philosophy by preparing his customers for the adjacent business with a generous dose of artery-clogging barbecue. The juxtaposition of dinner and death does reflect a certain Southern logic.

When business suffered from unkind word of mouth, Price was forced to close The Barbecue Barn. He was indignant about the gossip. "Why, they said I was barbecuing possum!" he railed. Unfortunately for him, that was the least of the talk. Rumors about what was actually in his barbecue gave locals flashbacks from the movie *Fried Green Tomatoes*. You recall that film: a bit of Southern Gothic cannibalism. One memorable scene shows the sheriff having his fourth plate of the tasty barbecue at the Whistle Stop Café during his search for the missing Frank Bennett, not realizing he has indeed "found his man."

The Summerville City Council will issue a permit if Mr. Price complies with all required codes. But Price is missing the point here. His aesthetic sense has suffered burnout from his previous failures. Barbecue and burials don't mix, even in Flannery O'Connor's home state, and you don't have to be a vegan to get it.

You have to wonder what he'll name his new establishments. One-Stop Crematory and 'Cue . . . or maybe Krispy Crem and 'Cue.

And you have to admire Mr. Price's persistence. Previous failure has not dimmed his vision of the ultimate shopping experience. So if you're traveling through Georgia and want to stop for a Southern snack . . . Oh, well. Never mind.

# Lake Wobegon South

I love small towns. Everybody waves at everybody in Livingston, Alabama. If it moves, you wave at it. It reminds me of my college days at Chapel Hill when, too vain to wear my glasses, I stumbled around campus in a blur, waving at all moving objects. I got the reputation for extreme friendliness when my behavior should have been chalked up to vanity and myopia.

Prisoners at the Sumter County Jail, right on the town square at the county courthouse, are taken out for an airing twice a day when the weather isn't sweltering. Some inmates amble around the jailhouse yard, while others sit in the mule-back chairs or hang on the cyclone fence, chatting with passersby and waving at cars.

My Mississippi friend, Knox, swore this was fiction when I told about the Livingston jail. She has since confirmed the story by cruising around the town square. Four prisoners greeted her with vigorous waves. She waved back, since it seemed the civil and courteous thing to do.

With small-town telephones, you have only to remember the

last four digits because the prefix is always the same. For the left-brain impaired and the aging, this is most helpful. I have become dependent on mnemonic devices, especially with numbers. Fortunately, my Livingston four-digit phone number is the date of my birth and my age: 1621.

In small towns, people let you cross the street even where there are no crosswalks. The department of transportation people, however, who seem to be the resident philistines in every state, put up bilious, oversized chartreuse pedestrian signs every twenty feet around the town square with the familiar symbol of the frozen walking stick man bent forward in everlasting haste.

The irony in all this is that nobody walks in downtown Livingston. It simply isn't done. You drive the half block to the P.O. In the olden days when I was courting and walking to town with my beau, curtains were pulled back from windows to see who was doing such an outrageous thing. Mama said I would have to stop going to town on foot. It was only two blocks from our front door to the Confederate statue at the courthouse, but it was causing entirely too much talk.

Train whistles punctuate the day here much as medieval bells must have divided daylight hours in the Dark Ages. The wail of the locomotive is part of the rhythm of the days and nights. The story goes that there used to be two express trains going through Livingston, the Doodle and the Through Doodle. They were regular as clockwork. You could put your skillet of cornbread in the oven when the Doodle whistled through and remove it when the Through Doodle roared past and your cornbread would be just perfect.

The most popular eatery in town is the Mennonite bakery, which serves carbohydrate-laden lunches bountiful enough to satisfy the hungriest plow hand. I guess the name "A Touch of Home" Bakery assuages the natives' guilt at the decadence of eating out so often and topping off every meal with Teutonic cobblers and cakes. The Mennonites close up the bakery for five days in July, which nearly 'bout sets off a wave of hysteria amongst the locals, me included. We head out to Tres Hernandos—otherwise known as "Mexico"—on the edge of town for Southern enchiladas until the Mennonites return. Livingston does love to eat out.

I like the cafeteria at the University of West Alabama. It has a milk machine with a chrome lever like an udder under a poster of a black-and-white cow, so you feel as if you are actually milking when you pick the skim milk selection. It adds a nice rural touch to a machine-age convenience.

Fast-food breakfast is popular here, too. At the local Hardee's, you plow through a flock of mockingbirds standing around the parking lot waiting for a bit of biscuit. In my coastal hometown, seagulls hang out on the asphalt at McDonald's. Birds seem more plentiful here, though that might be just my perception. They trill their songs before daylight and seem to sing and call all day long—jays, cardinals, thrushes, and especially mockingbirds. Harper Lee knew what she was doing when she made this ubiquitous Southern bird a symbol in her famous novel.

You know you are in Alabama when the Hardee's breakfast menu features a porkchop biscuit. Lake Wobegon South, a.k.a. Livingston, I love ya! Minnesota, eat your heart out.

# From the Bulletin

I write a lot about the small town of Livingston in the south-western part of Alabama. Livingston has become my personal Lake Wobegon, except that we don't do Lutherans here. Baptists and Methodists, yes, with a respectable clutch of Presbyterians thrown in. But no Lutherans. I will put my Southern small-town reality—where the men are clean, the women are well talcumed, and the children always go to Sunday school—up against Garrison Keillor's creation any day.

St. Paul's Episcopal Church is a tiny, beautifully maintained architectural gem. A Livingstonian told me that the church is well endowed, though I thought that usually referred to women rather than sanctuaries. I like to go to this circa 1842 church when I am in town. The ancient organist appears to be about eighty-five. A lady lurches in after he finishes his prelude to accompany him on the violin. Episcopalians are not breeders. The congregation is sparse, so I like to show up on Sundays to fluff out the crowd.

When I am not fluffing out the Episcopalians, I love to go to the Presbyterian church because of the minister. Against all odds, this ultraconservative church has embraced a lady preacher from Mississippi, a refreshing change from the usual and predictable Sumter County Presbyterian minister. She's a quilt maker and a wine drinker who sports a sterling-silver toe ring that flashes from her sandaled foot beneath her robe as she moves to the pulpit on Sunday mornings.

The Presbyterians tore down their lovely 1896 clapboard building some years back to erect a Colonial edifice that makes you think you're in Greenwich, Connecticut. Somehow, the stained-glass windows disappeared from the old Presbyterian church when it was razed. One story claims that old man McLeod buried them down by the Sucarnochee River and planned to dig them up in the dark of night for his own use. But old man McLeod died, and the windows never reappeared, and that was the end of that.

The Methodists covered their lovely 1884 clapboard building with vinyl siding several years ago. They don't like to talk about it.

The Baptists are the biggest congregation in town. The First Baptist Church I remember from childhood burned down. Rumor has it that it was burned by mistake because it had the same name as the black church down by the river. The story goes that one dark night, the KKK asked directions to the Baptist church and learned it was four blocks down the road. The outlaws rode past the black church by the river and through the darkened square and burned the wrong Baptist church on the other side of town. It's mighty hard to get lost in Livingston, population 3,530, so I think that's just a story somebody made up. That happens sometimes in Sumter County.

There were no Catholics and only one Jewish person in Livingston when I was growing up. Mr. Rosenbush, known to all as "Bush," ran the local hamburger joint. Those long-ago burgers reign supreme in my memory. Flossie was the lone waitress behind the counter, a friendly soul obsessed with Arlene

Dahl, an MGM beauty of the fifties whose trademarks were her strawberry-blond hair and her beauty mark. Flossie's wig missed Technicolor perfection, veering more toward cotton-candy pink. No beauty mark. I think Flossie was a lapsed Baptist.

Author Doris Betts says that songwriter Bob McDill knew how complicated our culture is and how central religion is to the South. McDill summed it up in his song "Good Ole Boys Like Me" by linking six fundamentals of Southern life: religion, race, family, storytelling, the "Wah," and hard liquor. He tells of a Bible-toting daddy giving his son a gin-soaked good-night kiss after a bedtime story of Uncle Remus and Brer Rabbit. A portrait of General Stonewall Jackson hangs like a religious icon on the wall above the bed. It's a Southern vignette put to country music.

The South remains a complex and contradictory world. I wouldn't have it any other way.

# Sumter Cinema

It qualifies as an unforgettable moviegoing experience. Your visit to the Sumter Theatre will be unlike anything you have ever tried. For a town of Livingston's size—less than four thousand souls, a population unchanged in the last twenty years—the theater is a multitasking center as eccentric as it is fun. Something between Zen and existentialism.

A thirteen-page xeroxed Sumter Theatre, Pizza & Discount Video/DVD booklet is delivered every week to local homes to keep customers up to speed on "Now Playing," "Coming Attractions," and the latest culinary offerings at the theater. The publication is a storehouse of information containing complete listings of all videos and games available, a menu with descriptions and prices, and miscellaneous information such as "The movie showing this week can be found in the *Sumter County Record-Journal* on the 'Attend the Church of Your Choice' page."

Sumter Theatre is a place where you can dine, rent a video, see a recent film on the silver screen, and get a school uniform shirt, a T-shirt, a sweatshirt, or a baseball cap inscribed (sewn or heat-pressed) with the lettering of your choice. Or you can bring in your own shirt for an iron-on patch while you browse the video rentals, trying to decide between *The Banger Sisters* and *Barbie as Rapunzel*. The sewing operation is a jumble of hats and shirts piled on a back counter behind the restaurant booths. This seems to be mainly a daytime activity. About suppertime, the place shifts its focus toward the big-screen feature and dining. This is when the action starts.

Signs are an integral part of the décor. Some are polite: "Theatre this way" and "Please put trash in the receptacle." Others tend to be edgy or borderline rude: "No loitering," "If you don't have anywhere to go, don't stay here," and "English is the official language of the Sumter Theatre . . . not mind reading."

Real bargains can be found in the video rentals. The spinning kiosks sag with new rentals at $2.52 and movies five months or older at $.99 . . . over a thousand titles for your viewing pleasure. Now, I understand the marketing ploy of $.99, but I'm still puzzling over the $2.52 new-movie rental fee.

The theater area itself is unremarkable, save for the oversized orange-and-brown-plaid Herculon couch against the back wall. "It seemed a shame to throw that good sofa out, and it works well here. It's a comfy spot perfect for large patrons or lovers . . . whoever gets here first," explained amiable Smitty Boyd, owner-manager of Sumter Theatre, Pizza & Discount Video/DVD. He really should rethink that name.

Film screenings have been delayed on occasion. Mayor Tartt once called and said that he and Mary were running late. Smitty held off starting the film until the mayor and his wife arrived and were comfortably seated.

Food can be ordered and eaten in the dining area next to the hats and shirts. Better yet, it can be delivered to you inside the darkened theater during the movie. (Note: This is *not* your usual dinner theater.) The food server—hunched over, a shadowy troll—patrols the aisle scanning each dark row of seats until he recognizes the customer and delivers the goods.

The menu? Specialty pizzas include the "Hungry Hunter," with four meats for the carnivores amongst us, and the "Tiger Tamer," designed for the truly famished, combining all the ingredients of the "Hungry Hunter" and the "Very Veggie." Fried catfish baskets, Cajun crawfish, Buffalo wings, BBQ, sausage dogs, stuffed jalapeño peppers, shrimp po-boys, funnel cakes. And with any burger, you get a choice of French fries or the Sumter Theatre's spec-i-al-i-tay . . . fried okra.

I went to see *Charlie's Angels: Full Throttle* and had a side order of those fried pods of the gods, brought to me in the middle of an exciting car chase. But let's face it, the whole movie is a car chase. Noshing on popcorn will never come close to munching piping-hot fried okra in the delicious dark of the Sumter Theatre's big screen.

# The Return of Steve Renfroe

Every county needs a larger-than-life legend, one whose image becomes part of the fabric of the community. Sumter County, Alabama, has such a person, whose life remains an enigmatic and curious reflection of his time and place.

Steve Renfroe galloped on a milk-white horse into the town square in Livingston, the county seat, late in 1868. The War Between the States had been over three years, Reconstruction was running its ragged course, and times were turbulent. What the citizens of Sumter County did not know was that the dashing Renfroe had deserted the Confederate army and was on the run for killing his brother-in-law in Butler County.

Movie-star handsome thanks to his blue eyes, his dark head of evangelist's hair, and his well-cut clothes, Renfroe was soon a major player in the social and political life of the community. In those hard times, it was rumored that Renfroe's white horse had been spotted leading the hooded riders of the Ku Klux Klan through the darkness in Sumter County. Sometime later, vigilantes killed two political agitators. Again, the leader was said to have ridden a milk-white horse.

But his rise to power proved the undoing of the stylish newcomer. He was elected sheriff of Sumter County in 1878, and that is when the popular law officer began to get bad press. Arson, blackmail, theft. He was said to have robbed his own sheriff's office twice and set fire to it to destroy municipal records containing evidence of his shady dealings. The sheriff, now an outlaw, was in and out of jail for the next five years, always managing to escape by charming his guards.

Livingston was no longer beguiled by the amiable ex-sheriff, but Renfroe seemed drawn to Livingston. After every escape, he returned to steal a horse from a citizen or rob money from a former friend or pocket a neighbor's flat silver. The citizens of Livingston wanted him out of their lives permanently.

On his last return, he hid out in the woods on the edge of Livingston until three farmers turned him in to local authorities. There was no escape this time. In the dark of night, footsteps and the voices of eight men were heard at the jailhouse door. The masked men tied Steve Renfroe's hands and led him south toward the Sucarnochee Bridge.

They stopped at a chinaberry tree, where the vigilante leader said in the ultimate irony, "We are all your friends, Steve. We are doing this for your own good."

Renfroe, never a churchgoing man, said, to the surprise of the group, "I wish one of you would say a prayer for me."

The leader bowed his head and said, "Lord, please rest this miserable soul."

Then they hanged the charming Steve Renfroe from the biggest limb on the chinaberry tree. The vigilantes chose the perfect tree for their grim purpose. The chinaberry blooms in late May, putting out impressive clusters of purple blooms. Its flowers are fragrant and seductive. But as summer wears on, the berries of the chinaberry tree—small, round, and yellow—prove toxic. By July, chinaberry trees are ripe with deadly fruit.

45

In the dark of night every July 13, they say, a rider with silver spurs on a milk-white horse clatters across the bridge over the Sucarnochee River and thunders into the town square in Livingston. The horse's name is Death.

# Get Thee behind Me

Since writing *Turn South at the Next Magnolia*, I have become a shameless marketer. Like those who sell Elvis portraits and Bengal tigers on velvet, I practically pull my car over, pop the trunk, and prop my books against the hubcaps or spread them over the hood for potential customers.

Road trips are a big part of book promotion. The best of them have been with my "Southern sistah," Celia Rivenbark, whose book was released the same time as mine. We had a hilarious gig on the *John Boy & Billy Big Show* in Charlotte, where we appeared as the Dumb Belles, unable to manage a presentable score on their famous quiz.

Billed as the Dueling Magnolias, we were now off for a three-city, four-day trip to South Carolina, where I lived for six years growing up. Celia was the designated driver. We drove through North and South Carolina, always carefully hugging the left lane, a good twenty miles an hour under the posted interstate speed limit. I'm old enough to be Celia's mama, had I been a child bride, but she drives like the thousand-year-old woman. I figure she's practicing up for her geezer years.

I had a hard time deciding what to wear for my evening as the senior Dueling Magnolia in my old state. I finally decided my Tennessee Williams white-linen number with the big *Sex and the City* silk peony was just the thing. Thank God it was after Memorial Day. I like to think of this ensemble as my Blanche DuBois look. Blanche after thirty years in the asylum, of course . . . on institutional food, a zillion carbs later. If the outfit didn't look okay, I was depending on the kindness of strangers to bite their tongues and not mention it.

Eventually, we got to the Meagerville area. We drove round and round on the highway. Like buzzards circling road kill, we knew the town was there, we just couldn't get to it. This may have been an omen. Finally, we found an exit and arrived at our bookstore.

Early for our reading, Celia and I ambled over to the snack counter. Most bookstores are generous about feeding authors who give readings. We had noshed on fabulous foccacia and portabello mushroom sandwiches and double cappuccinos and Thai tea in the past. The Meagerville bookstore gave each of us a single cookie and a lonely cup of coffee. After the readings were over, we sauntered back to the food counter. We thought we would upgrade that inadequate cookie to an apple gallette at $3.95 a pop. Let's face it, being a Dueling Magnolia is calorie-consuming work.

The counter lady said no. Apparently, the word was out. The authors had been cut off. No more handouts. We stood at the counter like overgrown Oliver Twists with pitiful looks that all but shouted, "Please, sir, we want some more." We had no more success than the fictional Oliver. We realized then that the natives take the name Meagerville very seriously. We disgruntled Magnolias scuttled off in search of a decadent chocolate fudge sundae at the golden arches.

As we were leaving town, we noted another unique feature of Meagerville. Roadside cleanup signs usually proclaim, "Helping

Keep Our Highways Clean," sponsored by the Jaycees, the Kiwanis Club, or other local do-gooders. On the Meagerville highway, the roadside cleanup sign said,

Helping Keep Our Highways Clean

The Church of Wicca

Witches . . . not that there's anything wrong with that. We were just amazed that witches were actually responsible for road pickup on that particular stretch of South Carolina highway. The idea was intriguing. Who knew that witches were civic minded? I wondered briefly if the lady at the bookstore dessert counter was a card-carrying member of the coven but dismissed that as an unkind thought. The mental image of crones picking up Sun-Drop cans danced in our heads. Celia and I regretted we couldn't hang out to watch the witches in action, but it was on to the welcoming arms of Columbia.

As we headed deeper into my old home state, a favorite quote from James L. Petigru kept rumbling through my head: "South Carolina is too small to be a country and too large to be a lunatic asylum."

# Schlepping through Georgia

I've stopped in lots of small towns on my summer trips to west Alabama, getting off the interstate and moseying along back routes, savoring the character of the tree-shaded villages. Several stops were deep in the heart of Georgia's *Gone with the Wind* country.

One time, I detoured by Social Circle, Georgia, so called because the gatherings around the town well made for an active community life. When Sherman left Atlanta, columns of smoke rising from the burned ruins at his back, he marched east through tiny Social Circle, which he rudely leveled with fire.

Sherman's scorched-earth policy left little from the 1860s except that well in the center of Main Street, around which all traffic has to flow even today. The well gets bashed from time to time by some drunk driver. The local historic society rushes out no matter what the hour, sometimes laboring all night to restore the well before dawn. Why the frenzy? Some philistines on the city council say the well is a traffic hazard and swear the next time it goes down, it will not be rebuilt. But the well continues to stand tall, obstructing traffic, daring impaired drivers, and giving the historical society its raison d'être.

Madison, Georgia, was not burned by Sherman and now boasts the largest historic district in the whole state. Greek Revival houses line almost every street. There are conflicting legends about the saving of beautiful Madison. One is that a local belle had met and corresponded with William Tecumseh Sherman before the "Wah." When the Federals were headed toward town, she rode out to beg that Sherman save her little town, and the general, having once been sweet on her, spared Madison. I don't want to denigrate the power of Southern womanhood, but this story just doesn't ring true. Take a look at Sherman's photograph. William Tecumseh was such an unshaven, ill-groomed Yankee that it's hard for me to believe a nice Southern girl in the nineteenth (or any other) century would have had anything to do with the likes of him, much less beg. Sounds like a revisionist chamber-of-commerce story to me.

Another version of the rescue seems more likely. Senator Joshua Hill, a classmate of Sherman's at West Point, heard of Sherman's march east toward Madison, hurried to the county line with a bucket of hot fried chicken, and pleaded for the town to be spared the torch. Now, here is something believable—the power of Southern fried chicken. We don't know if it was the friendship or the chicken, but the little Georgia community escaped the unkempt Sherman's burning sweep through Georgia.

William Tecumseh Sherman is not forgotten in these parts. It is a longstanding practice to use surnames as first names down South, a notion that is catching on all over the country nowadays. Though I know someone in the town where I live with the first name Sherman, I can't imagine any mama south of the Mason-Dixon line naming her baby boy that. It would be the same as naming the little fellow Adolf or Benito.

While crossing Georgia, I learned there are Alabama jokes. I know rival schools have such jokes. (Oscar, a family friend and engineering graduate from North Carolina State University, loves to tell Carolina graduates that when he rides through Chapel Hill, he has to be careful to keep his car windows rolled up. If he doesn't, he declares, someone might throw a Carolina diploma into the back seat as he drives down Franklin Street.) But I didn't know about rival-state jokes except that old saw about North Carolina being "a vale of humility between two mountains of conceit," the two mountains being Virginia and South Carolina, long known as a tad prideful among Southern states. The joke is that Georgia will soon have the largest zoo in the world. How is that, you ask? It plans to put a fence around the whole state of Alabama.

When I got back on the interstate after visiting Social Circle, I rode behind an eighteen-wheeler with mud flaps emblazoned with a Pappy Yokum creature in Rebel costume under the slogan "Sweet Home Alabama." I hummed my version of the Lynyrd Skynyrd tune as I passed the truck and headed toward the state line.

# *I Spy*

I'm an aficionado of spy stories, especially the real-life-female variety chronicling ladies who defied the accepted roles for women, crossed enemy lines, and led the kind of high-risk lives usually reserved for men.

It was Confederate women spies who really hooked me on the genre. Their counterparts on the Federal side seem to have lacked the *je ne sais quoi* of their Southern sisters. Union female spies tended to join the ranks and, disguised as soldiers, gathered intelligence for the North. Some, like Pauline Cushman, even ended up joining P. T. Barnum and touring the country like sideshow attractions—behavior entirely too public and unsavory for Southern sensibilities. The female Southern agent was a different sort. There were enough of them out there to warrant a political cartoon in an 1863 *Harper's Weekly* depicting a Confederate female spy dashing wildly through enemy lines on horseback but, ever the belle, riding sidesaddle in silk dress, hat, and gloves, carrying a valise exploding with Union army secrets.

Wilmington's own Confederate spy was Rose O'Neal

Greenhow. We call her our own because it was here that she met her end. A native of Maryland, she was passionate about the Rebel cause. Known since youth as "Wild Rose," she put her love for the South and her bent for adventure to use in espionage. Rose, a noted widowed Washington hostess, was said to have helped General Beauregard win the Battle of Bull Run (Manassas to Confederates) by giving him vital intelligence in a secret message. She had mastered a simple twenty-six-symbol cipher and had established a code with Lieutenant Colonel Thomas Jordan that transmitted information via the raising and lowering of shades on the southern side of her house.

First imprisoned in her own home under the surveillance of none other than Allan Pinkerton of detective-service fame, she was later incarcerated in the Old Capital Prison with her eight-year-old daughter. This proved a P.R. disaster for the Federals. It was much more damaging than any espionage information Rose transmitted. Even under prison circumstances, Rose still managed not only to entertain the elite of Washington but also to send out coded messages to the Confederacy, secreted in the fashionable hair buns and chignons of female visitors to the prison.

Later, the Yankees released Rose and exiled her to the South, an odd decision akin to throwing Brer Rabbit back into the briar patch. She arrived to welcoming applause in Richmond, literally wrapped in the Confederate flag. She later toured Europe, gathering admirers and substantial funds from supporters of the Southern cause. She published her memoirs, an *oeuvre* so theatric it resembled an overwrought work of fiction. Wild Rose adhered to the first rule of Southern storytelling: Drama always trumps truth. The memoirs became a bestseller despite the catchy title *My Imprisonment and the First Year of Abolition Rule at Washington*.

Rose then headed back to America—specifically, to Wilmington—aboard the blockade runner *Condor*. Inside her traveling outfit, hanging round her neck in a purse on a silver chain, were the proceeds from her book plus gold begged and borrowed from sympathetic European nobility, converted into English gold sovereigns worth about forty thousand dollars in today's money.

Pursued by a Union gunboat, the *Condor* ran aground at the mouth of the Cape Fear River. Fearful of capture, Rose and two others took off in a rowboat, but the small boat capsized. Burdened with the gold sovereigns, Rose sank like the proverbial stone into the black waters of the Cape Fear. The others in the boat managed to make it to shore as Rose disappeared beneath the waves.

The next day, a Confederate soldier found the drowned spy, relieved her of the gold sovereigns, and threw her body back into the river. When the corpse was found again and discovered to be the famous Confederate spy, it is said that the remorseful soldier returned the gold.

Her elaborate service was as close to a state funeral as Wilmington could muster during that dark war year of 1864. Lying in state in the chapel of Hospital #4, Rose O'Neal Greenhow's flower-strewn body was viewed by hundreds of weeping Wilmingtonians. That afternoon, following her funeral at St. Thomas Roman Catholic Church on Dock Street, her coffin, covered with a Confederate flag like that of a fallen soldier, was carried by Southern troops in a procession to Oakdale Cemetery. Every city dignitary was present. Rose would have loved the pageantry.

The forty-seven-year-old Confederate spy, the only female official war casualty on the Southern side, still sleeps beneath a marble cross under the moss-draped live oaks today.

# Those Zany Moon Sisters

.

Like the term *Southern feminist*, Confederate female spies were something of an oxymoron: women asserting themselves in the nineteenth-century patriarchy of the South and the unseemly, dark world of espionage. But they were good—very good, in fact—at their chosen vocation.

Especially the Moon sisters, unique in the annals of spy history: sisters spying for the Southern cause during the War Between the States. Originally from Virginia, sisters Lottie and Ginnie moved with their family to Ohio when they were young. They never got that Southern streak out of their system. Ginnie, the beauty of the two, is alleged to have been engaged to sixteen men simultaneously, writes Harnett T. Kane in *Spies for the Blue and Gray*. The lesser belle, Lottie, managed only twelve fiancés, the result no doubt of a less spectacular face described by contemporaries as "interesting." The use of the indifferent adjective *interesting* is cousin to the kiss-of-death, lackluster comment "She has such a good personality."

At the outbreak of the War Between the States, the Moon

girls were Southern sympathizers, or "Butternuts," as they were called in Ohio. They soon found ways of aiding the cause.

Lottie, once seriously wooed by future Union general Ambrose Burnside, the inspiration for the facial hair that bears his name, carried messages while disguised as an old Irish woman, brogue and all. The act must have been pretty good. The secret messages were delivered to Colonel Edmund Kirby Smith.

Beautiful Ginnie got into the act while still a teenager. In an Ohio boarding school at the outbreak of the war, she begged to be sent to Memphis to join her mother. She persuaded the head-mistress of the wisdom of her request by shooting out all the stars in the flag flying in the schoolyard, according to Kane. The youthful Rebel was sent packing immediately. Joining her mother in Memphis, Ginnie rolled bandages and helped nurse the wounded.

Sister Lottie had become a seasoned agent by that point. She easily crossed enemy lines by pretending to be an invalid, aided by her amazing ability to dislocate her jaw, thereby maximizing the pathos. The sound of the dislocation was said to be a fierce "cracking and grinding," which nailed the invalid act.

Lottie's adventures inspired Mother Moon and daughter Ginnie to travel on their own espionage venture from Memphis to Ohio on the pretense of visiting relatives. There, they were to gather military intelligence and badly needed medicine before returning home. All went as planned until, on the return boat trip south, the Moon women were identified as possible spies and threatened with physical search by a Union captain. Aware that discovery of the dispatches and medicines would prove disastrous, Ginnie went into theatric swoons and fantods, shrieking that they were personal friends of General Burnside (whom she had nicknamed "Buttons" back when he was courting her big sister). The captain beat a hasty retreat to rethink his plan. While he was regrouping, Ginnie whipped out the incriminating paper and reportedly "dipped it in a water pitcher and in three lumps swallowed it." Eventually, a woman called to frisk the

Moon ladies found that Ginnie was packing "forty bottles of morphine, seven pounds of opium and a substantial stash of camphor . . . all for medicinal use." Of course.

Under house arrest, Ginnie insisted that she be granted an interview with General Burnside the next day. Sister Lottie got into the act by showing up that day in the guise of a British aristocrat to try to persuade her old beau to release her mother and sister. Burnside recognized Lottie despite the disguise and promptly threw her in the hoosegow with the others. So much for lost love.

Buttons Burnside finally released the Moon ladies. Lottie's potent charm, even after all those years, melted her old beau's heart.

The Moons were put on probation for the duration of the war, although stories abound of other espionage antics. One tale says that Ginnie even traveled on the same train with Lincoln on one occasion. She was posing as a distraught Union widow accompanying her fallen husband's coffin home.

After Appomattox, Lottie returned to Ohio to become a journalist. Ginnie went home to Memphis and became, as many Southern ladies do, a full-fledged eccentric. She chain-smoked hand-rolled cigarettes (even in the Presbyterian church) and packed a pearl-handled revolver concealed in her umbrella, they say. After all, you never knew when you might have to make your point by shooting up a flag.

According to Kane, on one trip to New York, the elderly Ginnie, driving down Riverside Drive with friends, "glanced at Grant's tomb as they passed by. 'Damn him,' she said," puffing away on her cigarette.

As an old lady in Hollywood in the 1920s, Ginnie still had that Southern charm. She wangled several bit parts in movies like *The Spanish Dancer* and *Robin Hood*, featuring Douglas Fairbanks and Pola Negri. Unfortunately, all of Ginnie's roles were in silent movies. In the talkies, she could have been a contender.

# Retro Marriage Announcements

Don't you love wedding announcements from the early years of our last century? Your parents' or grandparents' newspaper clippings relayed every detail of dress, every last piece of appliquéd lace, and the exact rosette on the wedding cake. And all in passionate pink prose:

> The lovely Miss Lauren Ravenal Ladue in an exquisite
> custom-made gown of Alençon lace over cream satin
> with sweetheart neckline and the handsome Mr.
> Hastings McKenzie McPherson beamed as they happily
> left the rose-bedecked church as man and wife.

My friend Knox still brings me these clippings from Woodville, Mississippi, whenever she returns from a visit home. Woodville's journalistic style, thank goodness, has remained firmly entrenched in the kudzu and smilax of 1937. The write-ups are so excessive and sweet that your fillings will ache and your blood sugar rise.

The *New York Times* has taken the genre to new heights. The *Times'* wedding write-ups make those flowery, old-timey Southern wedding announcements seem absolutely Hemingwayesque. Another Alabama friend, a New Yorker for the past forty years, sent me wedding clippings and the *Times'* requirements when her daughter got married. Your odds on breaking into the *Times'* wedding section are close to your novel making the bestseller list. Many are called, but few are chosen.

The specifics are stringent. The *Times* wants to know the couple's names, addresses, schooling, and occupations. It wants noteworthy awards, charitable activities, and special achievements of the couple. It wants details on how the couple met. "Meeting cute," as they say, is crucial. The *Times* wants the name of the wedding official and his or her title. The residences and occupations of the couple's parents are requested, plus the telephone numbers of everybody remotely connected to the wedding. You have the distinct feeling that the *Times* requires the social security number of the wrangler for the butterflies to be released after the ceremony.

The photos have their own protocol. The *Times'* format now includes images of brides dressed in wedding gowns from the waist up, as well as informal photos of couples at home. It stresses that the images be of participants neatly dressed: "Couples should arrange themselves with their eyebrows on the same level and their heads fairly close together." These are the *Times'* words, not mine. I could never make this stuff up.

One couple met on an airplane. She gave him a ride home in her waiting limo at JFK. He sent thank-you flowers. Romance was afoot.

Another couple married in the same place where the bride had once lectured on her book, a tome on the way art mirrored the optimism of the Industrial Revolution, the *Times* tells us. One of this couple's early dates was to the photographer Weegee's exhibit of some of his best-known crime photos of the thirties and forties.

One prospective groom proposed in a gorilla suit, complete with clipboard with cartoon responses for the bride to check. The proposal ended with three singing Elvi in attendance.

One groom roomed with an iguana in college and was described as "zany." His bride was described as a "meticulous, petite woman with a waist no bigger than a pearl choker and the watchful nature of a Siamese cat, looking like a cross between Zelda Fitzgerald and Kate Moss in her grandmother's flapper-era wedding dress." Now, I ask you, can the *Woodville Republican* hold a candle to this deathless prose?

"The Times They Are A-Changin'," the song is titled. Does that include the *New York Times*? Aren't you gratified to know that the minimalist school of journalism is provincial and outré and that the *New York Times* has embraced Faulknerian prose?

# Songs from the Black Belt

For six weeks one summer, I researched and wrote at the University of West Alabama in Livingston. The area is known as the Black Belt for its fertile soil.

It seemed an eerie coincidence that Alan Lomax died just as I was leaving Sumter County, which is Lomax country. The father-son folklorist team of John and Alan Lomax is known by almost every person in the county. Without the Lomaxes, there would be no memory or record of the music and stories of this part of the South.

Research continues today on people the Lomaxes worked with, people who made their incredible contributions to American music possible. One friend of the Lomaxes was a remarkable person I remember well—Ruby Pickens Tartt, a tall, quirky woman, an artist who was outspoken and very different from most women in Livingston.

Miss Ruby grew up a daughter of privilege but broke out of the Southern small-town mold early on. Born in 1880, she graduated from college, studied art with the American impressionist

William Merritt Chase, returned to Livingston, and married a local suitor, Pratt Tartt.

Life changed for Miss Ruby in the 1920s when the author Carl Carmer came to Sumter County and enlisted her as an aide in his gathering of folk tales and superstitions from the black community. As a child, she had accompanied her father by carriage, bumping over dusty roads to the fields and cabins. She grew up admiring the rich music and imaginative folk tales of African-Americans. She became a familiar figure in the black community. Miss Ruby was invaluable as a liaison and source for stories and music because the singers and storytellers knew and trusted her. She was their friend. Carl Carmer fictionalized her as the character Mary Louise in his best-selling book, *Stars Fell on Alabama*.

During their visits in the 1930s, John and Alan Lomax rode with Miss Ruby into the Sumter County countryside. The Lomaxes lugged their cumbersome equipment with them to record their findings. Miss Ruby convinced the locals to sing and recite slave narratives and folk tales into the microphone for the strangers. The results were extraordinary. The Lomaxes recorded over six hundred songs from Sumter County alone—ballads, blues, work songs, play circles, field shouts. A treasury of the heart and soul of the African-American community.

Miss Ruby persuaded Vera Hall, a domestic in town, to sing for the Lomaxes. Hall's a cappella rendition of "Another Man Done Gone" is as haunting today as it must have been sixty-seven years ago when she sang into the clumsy recording machine at Tin Cup Alley in Livingston. With Miss Ruby's help, Vera Hall, Rich Amerson, and Dock Reed—all black folk-singing greats, all Sumter County natives—were recorded by John and Alan Lomax. I met Yale undergraduate Gabe Greenberg when he was in Sumter County that summer investigating Vera Hall, who died in the 1960s. Hall came into the limelight, he told me, when Moby combined her exquisite untrained voice singing "Trouble So Hard" with techno music on the album *Play*.

The graveyard in Livingston remains segregated, as it was in the nineteenth century. Separated by a fence on the ridge, whites and blacks sleep on either side of the hill overlooking the Sucarnochee River. Vera Hall was long dead by the time Ruby Pickens Tartt passed away in 1974. But old Dock Reed, another of John Lomax's discoveries and a friend to Miss Ruby, stood by the fence in the graveyard and sang the spiritual "Steal Away" at her funeral, his voice rising rich and full over the shaded gravestones at Myrtlewood Cemetery. There wasn't a dry eye on the hill.

# It's Time

My mama *never* changed her wristwatch as she traveled from one time zone to another. Visiting us in South Carolina, she persisted in Alabama time. When we were in Charleston's Middleton Gardens, she would look at her wristwatch and remark on how early it was for the gardens to be closing. Back at my house at 5:00 EST, she wondered aloud about our scandalous Mount Pleasant suburban habits. "Drinking wine practically midday!" came the mutter as she checked her watch. Yet again, we revisited the time-zone topic, to no avail. So we all had another glass of Chardonnay.

It was the same for daylight saving time, which I've just discovered I have been saying wrong my entire life. It is "daylight saving time," not "daylight savings time"—no *s* on saving. But I am sure only an aging English teacher or obsessive-compulsive grammarian gives a happy damn one way or the other.

Mama never acknowledged daylight saving time either and refused to adjust her wristwatch. "I run on God's time," she always said with a little huff. All Southern women are given to that huff, perfected early in girlhood. According to Mama, God did not believe in saving daylight and lived in the central time zone near the Mississippi line. Consequently, her watch was always accurate.

Mama wasn't the only one with a quarrel about the government's meddling in time. Daylight saving time has been on again, off again since its initial adoption in 1918 during World War I. Everybody hated it, so it was repealed after the war. It was reinstated in 1942, again for wartime, but was dropped again in 1945. For the next twenty-one years, everybody was free to do as they pleased, observing it or not. There was no national standard. Ironically, some politician in the sixties decided that since the government couldn't control bra burning or riots or hippies or Vietnam in those rebellious times, it could jolly well get a grip on time. It thus legislated the Uniform Time Act of 1966. Only in 1986 did we get a regular routine for establishing daylight saving time.

We all know the "Spring forward, fall back" mantra, which reminds us how to adjust the time on our clocks. But did you know that daylight saving time begins on the first Sunday in April and ends on the last Sunday in October? Neither did I. Mama may have been right. Somehow, all this regulation detracts from the poetic aspect of time—time that waits for no man, time whose winged chariot is always hurrying near—whether it saves daylight or not.

Time is ever the trickster. Sometimes, it stretches endlessly, defying logic and our own internal timepieces. Think of the minutes at the doctor's in that tiny examining room, alone, after you have left the convivial crowd in the waiting room. A small forever. Then, on occasion, time compresses. Yoga always does this for me. An hour-long class shrivels to four minutes. But the most interesting are those moments when time doubles back on itself and you are caught in the cosmic loop.

We had been invited to join another couple on their sailboat for a trip to Bald Head Island, where we would moor, enjoy a sumptuous dinner at a restaurant on the island, and spend the night on the boat before returning to Wrightsville Beach. But after hours of beating against a twenty-five-knot headwind, our captain said we would never make Bald Head before midnight and had better put in at Carolina Beach.

Ernie and I had never been to that community, so it was an adventure. Our hosts said that it wouldn't *exactly* have the same flavor as Bald Head Island but that we could get a taste of old Carolina Beach with its boardwalks, doughnut makers, colored lights, penny arcades, and great dirty-dancing beach music.

Jane and I, clad in our Bald Head Island shorts ensembles, sauntered out to reconnoiter the area for a restaurant. The men stayed behind to secure the lines, furl the jib, and other such nautical necessities. As we approached the corner across from the filling station, a red convertible crept along the curb and stopped just a little ahead of us. The two occupants, both middle-aged Fonzies, turned and leered our way. The Fonz nearer the sidewalk, a pack of cigs rolled in his sleeve, grinned. "You girls wanna go to ride?" he drawled. We "girls," both fifty-something, looked at the two sideburned prospects and then at each other. We burst out laughing. We whooped. We snorted. We all but fell out and rolled on the sidewalk in hysterics. We could not compose ourselves to speak.

The Fonzies were not amused. The convertible fled in a squeal of burning rubber. Little did they know that they had given two old dames a fabulous moment of time doubled back on itself. A step back in time. *Happy Days* redux.

# And Your Sign Is . . .

It's obvious that our present astrological signs, their origins obscured in the mists of antiquity, are outdated and should be replaced. It is time for a horoscope update with a Southern accent and real meaning. Similar horoscopes do exist on the Internet, but this is the real McCoy, given to me by my personal psychic, Rosetta Stone. After all, under our Southern skies, we may meet an occasional billy goat, the infrequent twins, even crabs on Wrightsville Beach. But virgins? Rarely, if ever!

What we need are down-home astrological signs: Southern signs. Pay close attention now to see where you and your loved ones fit into the new horoscope. Here we go.

December 23-January 20   Sign of the Mule
    You are the Arabian stallion of the South. You are
to the thoroughbred what Co-Cola is to Dom Perignon.
You have gained (unfairly) the reputation of being
difficult. Your determination is legendary. Besides your
work ethic, you have tremendous cultural influence.

You appear in every genuine Southern literary work, including those of Faulkner. Avoid relationships with hognose snakes. The two signs do not mix well.

January 21-February 19   Sign of the Pork Rind
You come from humble beginnings. You, however, can make something of yourself and rise above your social disadvantages, especially with the help of your mentor, Atkins. Always follow your gut feeling. Too much of a good thing can be hazardous to your health. Pork rinds are always at their romantic best with Co-Cola.

February 20-March 20   Sign of the Chigger
You are the most complex of the Southern signs and have an overwhelming innate curiosity. Your personality is such that you always get under the skin of those you encounter. You are never satisfied with the surface of things but feel compelled to dig deep. Marriage prospects, however, may be limited. Work on controlling your tendency to be tenacious and boring.

March 21-April 20   Sign of the Co-Cola
Ever popular, the Co-Cola flourishes in all seasons, is loved in a crowd, yet is outstanding alone. The best of its kind, the Co-Cola always beats out the competition and reigns supreme. You have been called "the champagne of the South," but don't let that go to your head. Use caution when partying with alcohol. You, Co-Cola, can always go the distance on your own merits.

April 21-May 21   Sign of the Hognose Snake
When confronted with life's difficulties, hognoses have a marked tendency to withdraw rather than confront problems head on. Your tendency to play dead is understandable but may be an inappropriate response. While this may be your way of meeting

strangers, your co-workers might call 911 or begin administering CPR. Your lethargic approach to life's problems may prove risky in the long run.

May 22-June 21    Sign of the GooGoo Cluster

You are the type who spends a lot of time lounging in a hammock and are frequently called "sweet thang" by those who know you well. Others consider you a bit nutty. Your rough exterior may present problems in your love life. This may be the year to consider water aerobics. On second thought, some other form of physical fitness may work better for you. A romantic match with a palmetto bug may be possible.

June 22-July 22    Sign of the Black-Eyed Pea

B.E. peas have a lucky aura around them. You love to get into the melting pot of life and share your essence with everything around you, though this sometimes lands you in hot water. Combined with close friends whose initials are H. J. and C. (hog jowls and collards), your New Year's Eve celebration is spectacular. You will always be the life of the party. In your personal life, stay away from those born under the sign of the Co-Cola. It won't work; save yourself a lot of heartache . . . and heartburn.

July 23-August 21    Sign of the Fiddler Crab

Since the fiddler is a Southern water sign, you tend to seek out those environments. Pluff mud and seawater are aphrodisiacs to you. Fiddler crabs prefer hot-tub dates to long drives in the country. Though found desirable by some, you may have difficulty maintaining relationships because you are often perceived as crusty. But it is well known that fiddlers are always good in a pinch.

August 22-September 23   Sign of the Watermelon

Your seeds of influence can be found in distant places. Summer is your time to shine and to find yourself the center of attention at social gatherings. You may appear cool to some, but your sweet self is difficult to hide. Because of your physical attributes, you are often a victim of harassment in the workplace. Beware of those who may inappropriately thump your bottom in passing. With watermelons, it is an occupational hazard.

September 24-October 23   Sign of the Hush Puppy

You are a follower, not a leader. Happy to accompany others, you excel at flattering your stronger companions. Some with heart problems, however, may fail to recognize your warm and tender inner self. They also avoid you because they find your personality too seductive to resist. Seek out those born under the sign of the banana puddin'.

October 24-November 22   Sign of the Water Bug (a.k.a. Palmetto Bug or Cockroach)

Water bugs are rarely popular guests, despite the fact that they mix so well. But you should be proud of your heritage. You have survived and flourished since the age of the dinosaur and feel at home in any setting, no matter how casual or formal. You dine with princes and paupers with equal ease. There may be a GooGoo Cluster in your romantic future.

November 23-December 22   Sign of the Banana Puddin'

The most basic of ingredients are key to your makeup. Although unpretentious, you are the sweetest of the sweet. This may be the most comforting of all the signs. You can hold your own in any elegant, cosmopolitan setting despite your down-home qualities. Remember, you have a great deal to offer just as you are.

There you have it. Read your horoscope. You can take on the day secure that your Southern sign will lead you down the right path and that your choices are in line with the planets. May your earth signs live in harmony with your water signs, and may your day be full of astrological wonders.

# Celebrate! Celebrate!

Little did I know that we have so much to celebrate. You may think October means only Columbus Day and Halloween. Wrong. We seem to have a day or a week or a month to celebrate just about everything.

In October, we have Grouch Day, Independence Day in Azerbaijan, Reptile Awareness Day, and Mole Day (strangely enough, a celebration of chemistry with the slogan "Rock and Mole!"). Then there's National Boss Day, Taiwan Restoration Day, Look Back on Your Life Day, Dictionary Day (take a dictionary to lunch?), and Bald Is Beautiful Day. And that doesn't count the weeks in October we celebrate: National Forest Products Week, Hepatitis Awareness Week, Save Your Back Week (celebrated by refusing to pick up teenagers' clothes, perhaps?). This doesn't even begin to touch the month celebrations: Peace, Friendship, and Goodwill Month, Caramel Month, Dinosaur Month, Pork Month, Fantasy Month, Healthy Babies Month.

I'm going to have to double up so I don't miss anything. It'll take serious multitasking. I'm whipping up a ham sandwich for a picnic lunch at the Cape Fear Serpentarium, so I can celebrate Pork Month on Reptile Awareness Day. I hate that I've already missed Older Persons' Day and World Smile Day and World Teachers' Day. Regarding the latter event, I'm hoping that my old-lady grin when I corrected one student's paper that talked about getting up "at the crack of darn" lets me off the hook.

Today, I'm finishing up Pet Peeve Week before I have to begin the Liver Awareness Month festivities. I'm winding up my Pet Peeve Week celebration with an Andy Rooney finale. I have developed my own Andy Rooney eyebrows run amuck but find it difficult to sustain the curmudgeon stance for an entire week. I'm fascinated that Andy has managed to make a career of being a grump. Only in America.

I will let you in on a few of my pet peeves. I can't stand rear car windows that don't roll all the way down. I can't abide geometrically pruned shrubs except at Versailles. I detest being called "you guys" by servers at restaurants and having my plate snatched away by the waitperson as the last morsel of food is lifted to my lips. You don't do that at home. It makes me look as though I've gobbled my meal, which I probably have. I deplore that I've been brainwashed to use the word *waitperson*.

I hate that my favorite lipstick, Juniper Sheer, has been discontinued and that I wasn't alerted in advance so I could stockpile it. And I hate that pointy-toed stilettos are back in fashion. I am furious when the TV movie runs the end credits in miniature type and then tilts them at a diagonal so yet another commercial can be jammed in on the right side and I can't read who that little blond ingénue was whose name I can't retrieve. I'm really ticked when my husband loses twelve pounds after three days on Atkins despite having supplemented the diet with peanut-butter-and-pickle-relish sandwiches when he feels he is having "a sinking spell."

Now that Pet Peeve Week is winding down, I'm making big plans for National Bologna Day. I'm cutting bologna sandwiches in the shape of pterodactyls, packing some Brazil nuts and Toll

House cookies, and reciting Sylvia Plath's "Sow" in our back-yard so I can knock off National Bologna Day, Dinosaur Month, World Food Day, National Poetry Day, Cookie Month, World Rainforest Week, and National Nut Day in one fell swoop.

On second thought, celebrating National Nut Day may cut just a little too close to the bone.

# The Ghosts of Christmas Trees Past

German immigrants brought the hamburger, ketchup, Levi's first blue jeans, the first hymnal and Bible to be printed in America, and the first kindergarten in the country, as well as a slew of talent: director Billy Wilder, Fred Astaire (born Frederick Austerlitz), Marlene Dietrich, and two presidents of German ancestry, Eisenhower and Herbert Hoover, whose surname was originally Huber. One of Elvis Presley's ancestors was Johann Pressler from Germany, according to relatives.

Most impressive at holiday time is that German immigrant, the Christmas tree. What else do we have that looks good, smells good, and instantly conjures memories of childhood delights and disappointments?

On our first married Christmas, I insisted we have a cedar tree. It was the central Christmas image from my childhood and the only proper Christmas tree in Alabama, I declared. My new husband informed me that in North Carolina, the correct tree was a spruce. It was early enough in the marriage that my lengthy sighs and baleful looks were still effective, so we got a cedar. It was scrawny and sparse, unlike the cedars of my recollection. The tree was so anemic that even the lightest ornaments bent its fragile branches to a sorrowful low. Despite the glittering ornaments, the tree appeared to be in mourning. It was our first and last cedar Christmas tree.

My grown children still complain about the 1976 Christmas tree. In a surge of ecological compassion, I decided we would have a living tree. This was no easy task in Mount Pleasant, South Carolina, where environmental indifference was especially high. Most nurseries suggested I get a metallic tree and be done with it. We finally found a white pine with a burlap ball that fit nicely into a galvanized tub. True, it was only thirty-two inches tall, but it would be splendid once we decorated it, and then we could plant it and every year gather around it and remember our bicentennial Christmas.

When we loaded the tree with ornaments, it developed a permanent starboard list from which it never recovered.

"It looks like it has tree mange," said my son.

"It can't support our angel topper. It keeps falling off," my daughter chimed in.

"It can take only one string of lights," said my Scottish husband happily. "Think what we'll save on electricity."

The children took to calling the tree "C. B." for the tree in the Charlie Brown TV special.

"It's alive, it's alive," I kept repeating. It was my Christmas mantra. "But it's alive!"

The children were not impressed. I realized I sounded like Dr. Frankenstein exclaiming over the first twitches of his man-made creature.

To my husband's credit, there was nary an I-told-you-so when we finally dismantled the forlorn tree. We planted it in the backyard. The children insisted we say a few words over it . . . as if the tree were the deceased at a funeral.

Every Christmas, we gathered round to see how the living Christmas tree had grown. It never changed expression. White pines do not like the Low Country. Every year, the pine appeared exactly as it had when we bought it, all thirty-two inches defiantly refusing to grow or to die. We finally moved away and left the stunted bicentennial tree behind, the only white pine in Charleston County.

I think the best Christmas trees blur into the years, indistinguishable from their predecessors. A few are unforgettable. May your next tree be full of sparkling lights and shining things and be beautiful and forgettable, fading into that collective memory of trees from the past. Merry Christmas and *danke schön*.

# Part II
## Brotheren

# Wear Mine

Corsages used to be everywhere—chrysanthemums at foot-ball games, roses on Mother's Day, gardenias at deb balls and proms. Now, they're a retro fashion fad. Faux flowers the size of dinner plates seem to be on every other shoulder.

The origins of the corsage are lost in the ether of time. I like to think some Neanderthal attached a couple of dandelions to the leather strap he used to hog-tie his lady love when he carted her back to his cave. Even he knew the value of saying it with flowers.

The earliest documented corsage reference I've found was in eighteenth-century France when Marie Antoinette, in her salad days playing shepherdess at the Petite Trianon, sported a corsage of potato flowers. It was an innovative use for a plant deemed at that time unfit for human consumption because it was a mem-ber of the deadly nightshade family and was not mentioned in the Bible. Shakespeare cited the potato as an aphrodisiac in *The Merry Wives of Windsor*, but it did not really take off until Marie Antoinette and Louis sprang the spud on the French court some years before the queen developed her unfortunate hankering for cake.

Despite Marie Antoinette's efforts, the potato-flower corsage did not catch on. Instead, Napoleon's passion for violets became the rage. He loved the little flower so much that Josephine had them embroidered on her wedding gown, despite the fact that her real name was Rose (Napoleon renamed her). The violet symbolizes faithfulness. Although that was not the couple's long suit (he divorced her after thirteen years), Napoleon did manage to send Josephine a bunch of violets every wedding anniversary. After her death in 1814, he picked violets from her grave and wore them in a locket for the rest of his life. Frankly, that bit of sentiment ranks high with me. It's about five clicks above minor accomplishments like the Napoleonic Code.

Back in my high-school days in Tuscaloosa, there were five or so spring dances, and orchids were the requisite corsage at every one. Those oversized purple numbers, when attached to a strapless evening dress, made the wearer glide with a starboard list. Every girl wore the hideous flower. We lurched rhythmically in a sea of bilious orchids on the dance floor to the tune of "Stars Fell on Alabama," always the closing dance.

My friend Naneita got a rare black orchid from her boyfriend our junior year. She wore it on a spectacular aqua dress trimmed with feathers. None of us had the heart to tell her the corsage looked like a giant wax flower pinched from some Dickensian mourning wreath. We assured her that it was fabulous and different. And in truth, it was both.

Mama, stunned that all of us girls got the requisite flower dance after dance, mumbled that none of us would have anything to look forward to as adults because of early-onset orchid madness. We would all be jaded demimondaines at age seventeen. She was right. To this day, I cannot look an orchid in the stamen. I did not know at the time that *orchid* is from the Greek word meaning testicle and signifies lust, greed, and wealth.

In Mama's youth in the Roaring Twenties, corsages were given to girls by beaux even at Easter. In 1927, Mama received three corsages of roses and lilies and carnations from three different fellows. One had a special note. My daddy's card said,

Baby, wear mine.

Howell

And she did. They married that August. Every spring for the rest of their lives, a corsage from the florist was delivered to our door on the Saturday before Easter. The enclosed card always had the same message: "Baby, wear mine."

# Sex and Aprons

I couldn't resist buying the poodle apron at the antique show for my daughter. White organdy with two appliquéd black poodles on long black rickrack leashes. Not a fashion item anymore, (maybe it never was), it is a collectible. Since I rarely cook, my purchase of an apron was strange. But this particular apron was more than an apron. For me, it was a ticket to the past.

It took me back to seventh grade at Hand Junior High in Columbia, South Carolina. There are not a lot of things I remember about seventh grade except I was crazy about a boy named Jack McConnell, our English teacher was obsessed with every gory detail of the Lindbergh kidnapping case, and I made an apron.

Miss Kinard's home economics was my least favorite class. In it, you had to learn to fix cinnamon toast, set a table, and make an apron from scratch before you were considered fit to be released into society at large and the eighth grade in particular.

Miss Kinard's tour de force was creating the apron. First came the pinning of the pattern. Oh, yes, there was a pattern. Then came cutting the material, pinning again, hand basting, machine basting, removing all basting, and finally regular machine stitching. It was a tedious, endless nightmare of stitching and ripping.

Every girl in that class can give you a detailed description of her apron fabric and design even after half a century. If you hated sewing when you started, you despised it by the time you finished Miss Kinard's class. Your material was so ratty and full of holes where stitching had been ripped out again and again because of some imperfect stitch that, upon completion, your apron hardly qualified for gift material. In theory, it was to be a Mother's Day gift.

My apron material was a Mexican print with a tiny sleeping man, sombrero tipped over his face, leaning against a cactus— all red, yellow, and green, and very politically incorrect. The trim was red rickrack for pocket and hem. Little did I know that this was a special form of torture for novice seamstresses. Instead of sewing straight across the rickrack, Miss Kinard made us sew up each tiny rick and down every tiny rack. "It will always lie flat that way," she said sadistically. I've had an aversion to rickrack and tacos ever since.

This class also taught sex education, or what passed for sex ed in that antediluvian time. We viewed an animated Technicolor film, the girls segregated from the boys. My recollection is that it was by Disney, but somehow I can't believe that Walt was spending his time after *Snow White* and *Bambi* producing sex-education films for seventh-graders in Columbia, South Carolina.

The only part I really remember is the dancing sperms, little animated creatures with canes, top hats, and spats who looked like multiple Fred Astaires. My friend Eleanor flunked and had to repeat the class. She passed "apron" but was mortified at the animated film, covered her eyes, and refused to view the little Fred Astaires. You'll be relieved to know that she is the mother of four grown sons and has a dozen grandchildren, so the damage was not permanent.

Another friend, Porter, experienced a more sinister classroom moment. She was locked in a closet with no lights for talking too much. As far as Miss Kinard was concerned, Dickens was alive and well, and she was a testament to that fact.

Years later, one of Mama's friends in Livingston, Alabama, gave me an apron shower right before I was married. I received dozens of them—dressy, whimsical, sporty, ruffled . . . a veritable trousseau of aprons. It must have been an Alabama thing. I've never heard of an apron shower before or since.

The Lindbergh case is no longer the crime of the century; Jack McConnell is dead, I've heard; sperm in sex-ed movies no longer wear top hats; and aprons are hardly considered a necessity. But this poodle apron will go on to a new life when my daughter wears it the next time she entertains. I like to think that it was made in Miss Kinard's class, but of course it wasn't. The black rickrack sewn straight across is a dead giveaway.

# P.E. Past

I'm not going to my reunion this spring at Tuscaloosa High School, and it's a big one. I figure that the next big one will have a skeleton crew of alums, pun intended, so I am sorry to miss this year's gathering. I especially wanted to see Miss Anna Brown, who was our senior English teacher. Every time I write the word *separate*, I think of Miss Brown. "Always put the *a* in for Anna Brown," she intoned in a voice like Eleanor Roosevelt's. And a hundred years later, I always do.

I do not remember a single teacher from P.E. class. It's a good thing I came along before the days of the girl athlete. Somehow, the misguided focus of my athletic endeavors was the costumes. It may stem from my days as a six-year-old tap dancer. For our dance recital, I was a blue-and-yellow satin daisy complete with sequined petal skirt and hat and fabulous silver shoes with one-inch metal taps capable of splendid cracking sounds. Like Truman Capote, I had dreams of growing up to be a tap dancer. It didn't work out for either of us.

Physical education was not my shining hour in high school.

You myopics out there will understand when I say that I avoided any sport that included the use of a ball. Any sphere hurtling toward nearsighted me brought instant panic, my arms raised to protect my head. I was never the first choice on any team, since I couldn't catch the ball, since I had no hand-eye coordination, and since I could never throw it within twenty feet of the receiver. The only game I like involving a sphere is croquet, in which the ball is already safely on the ground.

Besides my aversion to spinning balls, there was the fashion issue. We girls were required to dress in hideous one-piece bloomer outfits. It was part of the important lesson of conformity, I guess. The first fashion offense: color. All uniforms were a bilious royal blue last worn successfully by the Supremes. The second offense: style. The belt was buckled by a chrome double circle that cinched the bulky outfit at the waist and made even the slimmest wearer resemble a sapphire flour sack. It was, however, a democratic fashion equally unflattering to all who wore it.

My freshman year in college, in an attempt to escape ball sports, I took fencing and learned that Douglas Fairbanks and Errol Flynn deserved every swashbuckling penny they ever earned. Fencing is a wonderfully choreographed sport with civilized patterns of movement designed to give you the muscled legs of a javelin thrower. But fencing requires not only strategy and skill. It requires courage. I became an expert at the parry, a.k.a. the defensive move. Retreat, parry, parry, retreat. I was the Bert Lahr of the fencing class, without the cowardly lion costume.

The fencing outfits, by the way, were quite wonderful, except for the chest protector. The sleek white fitted pants and jacket and the screened mask made you look like a white bumblebee, the epee being your stinger. The padded chest protector didn't do a lot for your figure, but the fear factor made it an indispensable part of the ensemble.

At Chapel Hill, I was a modern dancer with black leotard, Capezios, and a veil skirt. I was easily the best falling leaf in our class, collapsing beautifully onto the floor, veil flowing and swirling around my lowered head, hands artistically crumpled, an image from the film *The Red Shoes*.

These days in my water aerobics class, fashion is not a factor. I am well over the satin-daisy and royal-blue-gym-suit days and am content, even pleased, to execute the rocking horse or frog leap in my faded old Jantzen. I think I've *finally* got it. Talk about your slow learner.

# Lions and Tigers and Grits, Oh My!

Dear Slipping Seniors Rest Home,

I am writing to reserve a suite at your institution for my husband and me. We qualified for the senior-citizen discount ages ago and feel we are well suited to assimilate into your special population. We understand that you use therapy dogs brought in to interact with the inmates. Please exclude us from that particular service, since an animal is largely responsible for our need to enter your care. Coals to Newcastle, so to speak.

When my husband had a heart procedure recently, I thought a puppy might be good therapy for a speedy recovery. We had been dogless for several years and have an aging cat named Sumter who, frankly, is disinterested in being a therapy pet and remains her usual aloof, indifferent self. In other words, she is pure cat . . . just one can of Whiskas away from being feral.

We found a West Highland terrier puppy that

seemed a good candidate, since size is a major consideration for our aged backs. Fifteen pounds is our limit without sending us into our emergency supply of Bengay. The little dog was eight weeks and five pounds when we got him. We settled on the name Grits, since the Westie is white and we wanted a Southern name. My husband was quite excited about the literary possibilities of the name, envisioning book titles like *Me and Grits, On the Road with Grits, Grits Goes to Vegas, The Gourmand with Grits,* ad nauseam.

Like childbirth, owning a puppy is an experience that mercifully fades from memory with time. Without that amnesia, there would be no newborns or puppies in any household on the planet. The chewing, the potty problems, the shredded papers, the chewing, the disassembled sneakers, the sleep deprivation . . . and did I mention the chewing? Then there is the constant whining, crying, and yelping . . . not to mention the noises the puppy makes.

The innovations since we experienced puppyhood in the 1970s are crate training, scented puppy pads to .encourage potty training in a designated spot, puppy preschool (Grits is already enrolled in the most prestigious of these), strobe-light attachments for collars, and stores where the animals shop right along with their masters. We have adjusted to these changes. It is the exhaustion factor we did not figure on.

A Westie is a cheeky little dog, full of spunk. Remember Lou Grant's comment on *The Mary Tyler Moore Show* when he first meets Mary Richards?

"You've got spunk," he says.

Mary lowers her eyes, smiles, and nods.

"I hate spunk," Mr. Grant says.

I agree with Mr. Grant. Spunk is vastly overrated. Grits is a tireless retriever and has the climbing instincts of a mountain goat. Bred to hunt Scottish vermin such as weasels and badgers, and not finding them readily available in the Low Country, Grits consumes moths, stink bugs, and cicadas with the gusto of a short, furry Hannibal Lecter.

We have set up a modest trust for Grits, if the children are agreeable to the terms. If convenient, we will arrive at the Slipping Seniors Rest Home tomorrow in time for the cocktail hour. We are both partial to Xanax on the rocks with a twist of lemon. You will recognize us by our valise missing a handle and our airline bag with a hole chewed next to the left wheel. We will be the ones whimpering, "Lions and tigers and grits, oh my!"

# Here Kitty, Kitty

In sorting some old photos recently, I paused over one taken years back in Raleigh. That was three cats and two dogs ago, if you mark time the way I do. It was a snapshot of Bullet, our Maine coon cat, perched in the pantry atop a white plastic pail of Happy Song birdseed, looking directly at the camera, waiting (it appeared) for some stray Carolina wren to wander into his clutches.

The pose also brought to mind our previous cat, Sydney, an extraordinary-looking Persian, the Johnny Depp of our menagerie, who trained himself to use the potty in our powder room. I see ads from time to time for contraptions you can attach to the toilet seat to assist your feline friends in becoming potty-trained. But Sydney was self-taught. He learned in the trenches, so to speak. After a surgery left him with stitches bisecting his shaved belly, Sydney was put in our guest room with food, water, and a litter box in the small adjoining bathroom. In the following forty-eight hours, the litter box was undisturbed. We grew alarmed. A quick trip to the vet assured us that Sydney was going somewhere and that there were no urinary blockage problems.

The cat had for some unknown reason begun to use the human litter box instead of his own. It was a wondrous and remarkable turn of events. This habit lasted throughout the rest of his life. And I can tell you that a cat without a litter box is like a day without . . . well, you can imagine the plus side of this talent.

Guests at our house, however, especially at parties, would return from the powder room lily faced, some clutching their hearts. They had entered the loo only to encounter Sydney, in all of his seventeen-pound Persian glory, perched on the seat of the john. It was a visual heart stopper. Bladder problems became rampant amongst our friends.

Sydney's good looks gave him notoriety in our Camp Lejeune neighborhood. He was once spotted in noisy attendance at a love-in at a neighbor's quarters right behind our house in Paradise Point. A corporal knocked at our door, cap in hand, and said our cat was a reported offender at Colonel States Rights Jones's house, three doors down. (Colonel Jones was from Mississippi.) Cats were everywhere, yowling under shrubs, lounging on porches, caterwauling, hovering on the fences. "Are you aware," he asked politely, "that a second pet offense could cause you to be expelled from Camp Lejeune housing?" The corporal explained that Sydney was the only cat specifically identified by an eyewitness. Large, handsome, silver-gray, bushy tail—the cat, not the eyewitness. So much for extraordinary good looks. The plain-vanilla alley cats ran off scot-free to woo another day. Sydney got a ticket to ride—straight to the vet to lose his manhood and his penchant for romancing the colonel's Siamese.

We never had another cat that was potty-trained. We returned to the world of cat boxes, newspaper, and kitty litter with our next feline.

My husband and I have talked about the personalities of cats who have owned us in the past forty years. I claim that

Sydney was the smartest of the lot, since he potty-trained himself. Ernie always says he doesn't think the cat was *that* smart.

"Why not?" I ask.

"Well, he never did learn to flush," he shrugs.

# Foaming at the Mouth

The advent of the West Nile mosquito virus in Louisiana and Mississippi made us all edgy. The July news from North Carolina really caught my eye. "Rabid Cat Attacks Three People," the headline read in the *Raleigh News & Observer*. Even more alarming, the rabid cat in Raleigh was a house pet current in her rabies shots. "Nothing is foolproof," the public-health vet said reassuringly, according to the newspaper. The cat attacked its owner and a next-door neighbor, who said it leaped at him from eight feet away. The cat assaulted another neighbor the next day. The cat's name, oddly enough, was Sweet Pea.

And why my interest? Yogi Berra was right. It was déjà vu all over again. I had my own rabies scare in Alabama during my six weeks' summer stay in Sumter County. It began on a balmy evening when a friend and I sliced up some gorgeous Better Boy tomatoes for BLT sandwiches. We decided that the back steps of the historic circa 1835 Moon House, where I was staying, would be a perfect spot for supper.

The yowl of a cat by the old pecan tree was plaintive but

strong. "Hey kitty, kitty," I called. The tabby, a very tall cat with long, black vertical stripes on his legs, slithered out of the shadows and waited. I pulled a piece of bacon from my sandwich. The cat ran to me. As I held out my offering, the cat clamped down not on the bacon but on my hand. So much for sharing a BLT with a stranger. It was a nasty bite, a deep, wide wound. The cat took off into the night when I hollered.

The next day, the doctor gave me an antibiotic prescription and advised capturing the cat to check for rabies. A local police officer and I set out a Have-A-Heart trap. For a week, I captured cats: preteen orange cats, elderly gray cats, calico cats, but not the feral striped tabby that had taken a hunk out of my hand.

I talked with the health department; I talked with the Alabama epidemiologist in Montgomery; I talked with the vet; I talked with my doctor. The news was troubling. No, there had not been an incident in Sumter County in some time, but nearby Pickens County had rabies so often that the authorities had an air-raid siren they set off. The long wail warned residents to take to high ground because there was a rabid animal about. Think *To Kill a Mockingbird*. Mississippi—we were a heartbeat away, practically on the state line—had some rabies cases, but of course, there was no getting around the unkind cracks about those natives foaming at the mouth.

Rabies was not likely but was always a possibility. And once you develop symptoms, it is too late. You are a goner.

The doctor said, "Percentage-wise, the chance for rabies is slim. Of course, you can pray."

I thought about my favorite Middle Eastern maxim: "Trust in God but tie your camel." I told her that I did not care for the odds. I still had a few things I'd like to do.

One local asked me if I were sure it was a cat. "Sometimes, things are not what they appear to be," she whispered ominously.

I pondered this and knew I was home, a place where superstition mixes freely with the ozone.

I thought about poor Edgar Allan Poe, whose strange death

at age thirty-nine in Baltimore has in recent years been attributed to rabies. His raving hallucinations, violence, aversion to water, and spiking fever preceding his death led some forensic scientists to propose the posthumous diagnosis. And he had cats, the most famous being Catterina.

I did get the series of rabies shots, which wasn't bad. The plus side is that I am now immune for life. This opens up all sorts of career possibilities. Raccoon wrangler for wildlife movies. Bat purveyor for vampire films. Backup for the dogcatcher. I'm ready, should the opportunity arise.

On hot summer nights, I still dream about a tall cat with an ungodly yowl and black tuxedo stripes on his back legs . . . searching for a stranger with a BLT.

# Bitty's Birthday

It was a big birthday for my sister. A *realllly* big one. If I told you which birthday this was for her, I'd have to kill you . . . or myself. The birthday party was held in the Chapel Hill Museum, but I doubt my sister saw the irony in this.

Squeaky, the hot-dog man, usually found selling his wares and chatting it up with the famous Chapel Hill flower ladies at his stand by the bank on Franklin Street, catered the birthday supper. Squeaky's cart and umbrella had been squeezed through the museum doors and set up for the entrée: hot dogs all the way . . . slaw, chili, onions, the works. And of course, another option: vegetarian hot dogs with vegetarian chili. After all, this was Chapel Hill. Cokes, chips, veggies, and cake completed the menu.

The food was unique, but the entertainment was spectacular, a perfect fit for my sister, whose name is . . . Bitty. The entertainer, Mark Andrews, a.k.a. Chicken Man, arrived with his family (Chicken Woman and Chicken Girl) and his troupe of trained Japanese silkies. Those chickens were exquisite enough to make

Martha Stewart—longtime breeder of Araucana chickens, which produce *pastel-colored eggs!*—swoon with envy. Chicken Man drove his feathered friends from Raleigh in his specially outfitted red truck. Thankfully, the poultry could not read the sign painted on the vehicle's side: "Warning! A Chicken May Be Driving This Truck."

Mark Andrews's chickens came home to roost some years ago. That's when he began touring with his world-famous silkies. He and his chickens perform for birthdays, rehearsal parties, reunions, bar mitzvahs, and wedding receptions—wherever and whenever an imaginative party giver calls.

Andrews, in his forties, is an admitted born-again chicken man who despaired of ever having a partner to share his life. He prayed daily for a helpmate to be sent to him. At one show, a woman stayed after his performance. "I like your chickens," she said. Thirty days later, the new bride marched down the aisle with four Japanese silkie bridesmaids in attendance. Chicken Man had found his Chicken Woman.

During the performance, one silkie sat on a high chair, one rooster perched on a dollhouse, and another, Aquilla, did a credible job of playing dead when Chicken Man said he was going to wring her wildly wildly wildly wildly scrawny neck. No dog ever played dead with more conviction. When dropped in a large stew pot, Aquilla reappeared as a dead plucked chicken. Turned out it was a rubber chicken. The sleight of hand was pretty convincing. One less-talented chicken, Apollos, added and subtracted at the prompting of Chicken Man. The mathematical fowl pecked the microphone and clucked to give its answers and subtracted wrong only once . . . not one of your more sensational animal routines.

My pedestrian concern was for the museum floor, but I was informed that the white silkies were housebroken. Besides, they would be on their custom-made cart at all times. This turned out not to be the case.

Chicken Man announced his birds would act out stories, minidramas, some biblical in theme. I was hoping for a reenactment of the Prodigal Son. But the winter storm and mounting snowfall cut the evening's entertainment short.

For the grand finale, Priscilla, one of the silkie headliners, rode all over the museum in a red remote-control car. Weaving among exhibits and display cases, her jaunty white topknot of feathers like a pillbox atop her head, Priscilla seemed the Rosalind Russell of chickens: elegant and sophisticated. The only thing missing was the princess-unscrewing-the-light-bulb wave. A hundred guests clapped and cheered.

We drove back to Cary, the snow coming down heavily now, visions of Aquilla and Priscilla swirling in our heads. We thought about stopping at KFC for a snack to go. But we didn't. Somehow, it just didn't seem fittin'. We noticed that the lights flickered and then went dark on the KFC building as we passed. And we were glad.

# Das Boot

Oprah's live-in-the-moment philosophy proclaims that accidents happen to make you slow down and pay attention. God knows, I thought I *was* paying attention. I certainly am now. No need for a high-drama event to deliver that message.

I've done it again, breaking a bone in my left foot, some years after my spectacular triple break in the same leg. The only fun part has been coming up with a name for this piece. Old cinematic titles like *Das Boot*, *My Left Foot*, *Forrest Gimp*, *They Shoot Horses, Don't They?* and *Misery* come to mind. All presume my predicament to be screen-worthy, though in truth it isn't.

Like Zelda Fitzgerald, I have taken to hurling myself down flights of stairs. My left leg seems to have developed a death wish. A friend told me his physical therapist believes a hurt leg makes the well leg jealous. After all, the hurt leg is favored in every way. Everyone rushes to slip a pillow under it. It is pampered. The well leg gets "leg envy" and manages to have an injury, too, so it will get the attention and care the wounded leg receives. Of course, this philosophy may not hold up under scientific scrutiny.

I recently broke the pack rat's cardinal rule: Do not throw anything away. You may need it down the road. As soon as you dispose of an item, you'll certainly have use for it. I cleared out a closet and decided the 1993 full-leg orthopedic boot had to go. The thing was just too bulky to deserve a place amongst the twenty-two years of *National Geographics*, the Citadel cadet's parade hat, and my collection of S&H Green Stamps books I'm saving for final redemption.

I should have known better than to give that orthopedic boot away. That is the rule of the jinx. It works on the same principle as baby equipment. You give away a baby crib, you get pregnant. Give "Das Boot" away, you break your foot again. But at least you don't get pregnant.

I guess I'd hung onto the boot out of sentimentality. I had worn the device to my son's wedding. It was a real fashion statement with its pewter rotating joint and black plastic case up to my knee. It gave my silk MOG dress—that's mother of the groom—an unfashionable bulk around the knee. Months later, I ended up returning the boot to my orthopedist in the hope that some other hapless soul could use it. Since it was the most expensive single piece of footwear I had ever owned, recycling it appeased my Scot's heart.

However, I did not disturb the arsenal of other accouterments hanging on our garage wall like trophies from some orthopedic safari. Among them are two pairs of crutches, one for a very tall unfortunate and the other for a Tiny Tim, left I guess from one of our children's skateboard accidents. Hanging between the weed whacker and the pressure-washer extension is a walker remaining from my last mishap, after I failed to master the crutch. Its fleece handles are worn and drab from the long, dusty exile in the garage.

And how did I manage to break my foot? Fell off the last step to the sidewalk at Kenan Auditorium at the North Carolina Symphony. Soaring on Brahms and Tchaikovsky after the concert, I sailed from the bottom step like a diver going for a half gainer.

"At the symphony!" sniffed my friend Celia, exasperated.

"If you had been home watching *Survivor* on your TV like you're supposed to on Thursday night, it never would have happened," she cracked.

# For the Birds

Granddaughter Caroline, when almost four, found a fledgling robin in her backyard. She christened the baby bird Spika, a name more suitable perhaps for a chicken hawk but a moniker that should have given the tiny feathered thing a boost of confidence.

Carolina wrens, not robins, are our problem. We call these wrens the Forrest Gumps of the bird world. They really don't get it. They find themselves in the most amazing places and situations and are so clueless that they repeat the death-defying acts spring after spring.

Years ago, we discovered atop a nail box in our garage a wren nest containing three featherless babies, mouths yawning wide in a perpetual plea for food. We monitored them carefully every day, watching as they grew to fledgling stage, the wren parents flying in and out of the garage to feed them.

Our Maine coon cat, Sumter, also monitored the bird nursery and even took to lying on the top of the car to get a wicked eye-level view of the nest activities. One morning, no wrens darted in and out of the garage. We found Sumter curled on the back-door mat beside the body of a bird whose tiny wren feet pointed straight up in the air. The other wren parent was nowhere to be seen. The bird widow or widower had decided that discretion was the better part of valor and hit the road. The orphaned fledg-lings had been abandoned.

This called for drastic action. The baby birds would starve or, even worse, fall into Sumter's waiting jaws if they tried to fly from the nest. Our vet gave us the name of a wildlife rehabilita-tor. This incredibly kind woman came right over, put the nest with the chirping baby wrens in a shoebox, and drove away.

I called the next week to check on our babies. The rehabili-tator said she had gone to a wedding in Winston-Salem over the weekend and taken the birds with her. She had left them in the motel room in the shoebox, returning every three hours to feed them. No mama wren could have been more devoted.

Now, every spring when wrens try to nest in the garage, we remove the straw and leaves before any eggs appear. But one year, they outsmarted us. By the time we found the nest in the grapevine wreath hung high in the garage, it had four newly hatched babies in it. We were due to go out of town for over a week. My son got the bird duty, making sure Sumter did not make lunch of the new family. The happy litter of wrens sur-vived and flew away to build nests of their own.

While some of our feathered friends are the Forrest Gumps of the bird world, others are escapees from Edgar Allan Poe. Re-cently, a pair of huge, dark birds swooped over the deck and landed on the railing. At first, I thought they were pileated wood-peckers, which we've seen twice since we moved here. I called my husband and grabbed the binoculars to get a better look, but magnification was not necessary. The two were perched on the wide deck rail, peering into the screen porch, straight at us.

They were not pileated woodpeckers. They were not wrens or mockingbirds or blackbirds or any of the usual suspects. They were turkey buzzards, perched as calmly as canaries, serenely staring us down. Until you have been glommed by an enormous buzzard, you haven't been given the evil eye. In all my bird-watching years, I had never been so close to these creatures.

Eventually, the buzzards flapped their mighty, dark wings—their flight akin to a loping gait—and landed in a nearby magnolia, where they lingered for almost an hour. Following our noses, we found by the back steps the dead possum that had lured them to the deck. Once we got rid of the possum, the buzzards abandoned their vigil.

You won't hear us complain about our Forrest Gump wrens anymore. Those foolish birds and their ill-advised nests will be a welcome sight when we recall their ominous, dark brothers looming over the back deck.

# Joint Camp

In the dead of winter, I returned from four days at Joint Camp. Not the season? This Joint Camp meets year-round. A bit old for a camper, you say? If you could meet the other campers, you'd agree that I am the youngster of the group. I know, the name Joint Camp conjures up visions of elderly campers huddled around a campfire smoking stubby joints from roach clips . . . and inhaling. It's an unsettling vision at best.

But the orthopedic Joint Camp at Cape Fear Hospital was in a special wing set up for us campers having knee or hip replacements. There were seven other campers: three other knees and four hips. Most had operations the day before starting camp, but one had his a day earlier. This time line becomes important later in the story.

Our orientation was scheduled for the Wednesday a week before surgery, so we could learn the ropes and meet the other campers. I fretted that I would not have my nametags sewn in the waistband of my underpants in time. It turned out I was the only camper at the orientation.

"I'm disappointed. I was hoping to meet my fellow campers, sing a couple of choruses of "Kumbaya," make s'mores, and
roast weenies," I said to the nurse.

"I can't do anything about the singing or the s'mores, but
we do have a couple of weenies coming by to see you," she
winked, nodding toward one of the doctors coming toward the
room. I hoped *she* was going to be my camp counselor.

Twenty-four hours after the knee replacement operation, my
large reclining chair and I were rolling down the hall toward the
Joint Camp room—called "the Clubhouse"—for our first meeting. We knee patients all sported hideous TED stockings on the
legs with our new knees. Heavy, thick white compression stockings. I thought TED might stand for Ted Turner, Ted Danson, or
Ted Kennedy, possible developers of the world's ugliest stockings. Turns out it is an acronym for thrombo embolism deter-
rent. TED stockings are the least desirable hosiery since paint-on
seams during World War II. We tried to think of them as dancers' leg warmers, but the ruse didn't work.

We campers were divided into the green team and the blue
team. I had not known this was to be a competition. In something of a Percocet haze, I joined the other campers in a circle.
We watched demonstrations of the intricacies of walkers and
crutches. We practiced maneuvering across the floor. We practiced negotiating pseudo-stairs. We talked about "recovery
friendly" homes. We talked about diet. I desperately hoped the
singing would start soon.

One of the campers was having a reaction to the anesthesia,
hurtling toward the door every few minutes to reach the bathroom. Though I dubbed her "the Barfer," I felt sorry for her dis-
comfort. Another hip patient on the blue team, and I'm not
referring to his mood here, had his operation a day earlier than
the rest of us. He was very full of himself and all but tour-jetéed
across the floor in his walker. He pranced up one side of the
practice stairs and down the other with a flourish. He preened
across the floor back to his rolling bed. Our collective loathing

was palpable, even amongst those of us most pharmacologically challenged. Mumbles from the campers about possible short-sheeting under cover of night bounced around the room.

That evening, both the green and blue teams were in a mutinous mood over supper and later at the movie *Legally Blonde*. We picked at our special camp food lethargically and sneered at the screen image of the perky Miss Witherspoon.

The next morning, the campers met for a lesson on car transfer. The cocky hip patient had suffered a bad night. He arrived snarling in his rolling chair; the bon vivant had vanished. We all smiled. A communal gloat settled over the green and blue teams. There was justice in the world. Our camp *joie de vivre* returned.

I'm thinking about having a big birthday bash for my new knee to celebrate its first year in the world. I request no gifts, of course—just the presence of your company to raise the glass and toast my good doctor, the counselors of Joint Camp, and a bionic knee. Do come!

# Leafers and Lovers

Several Octobers ago, my husband and I decided that another autumn could not pass without heading to our North Carolina mountains. We became part of that flock that migrates to the Smokies, the "leafers" who take to the hills to soak up the gorgeous foliage. Armed with camera and binoculars, we found a room in a former tuberculosis sanatorium from the early 1900s, a hard-won accommodation during peak season in Buncombe County. It was hard not to think of those poor "lungers," as the old-timers called TB patients, when we pulled up at the bed-and-breakfast and saw that the most distinctive architectural feature was the large glassed-in porch where long-gone patients had soaked up the sun at the turn of the century.

Though married for a millennium, my husband and I had never stayed at a bed-and-breakfast. We arrived at dusk. The inn was cold and dark, straight out of Dickens's *Bleak House*. Our hostess informed us that the furnace was on the fritz, but that they were "working on it." My husband did not think the downstairs temperature to be "rustic and charming," as advertised in the brochure.

"Long on the rustic and short on the charm," he grumbled as we schlepped our luggage upstairs to our room.

That room, labeled the "Sourwood Suite," was less than spacious. The double bed occupied 87 percent of the floor space. We stood side by side, wedged between the wall and the bed, and surveyed our digs. A narrow pathway enabled us to navigate sideways around the bed, like human crabs, over to the chifforobe. There was no closet. We are both of average height, but when I tried to hang our clothes, I realized that the anachronistic 1920s Grand Rapids wardrobe was designed for Jazz Age pygmies. My dresses hit the floor of the chifforobe right above the knees, while Ernie's trousers crumpled at mid-calf. We were refugees from *Gulliver's Travels*.

The bedside lamp was an obvious problem. It was what is cunningly called a "*Gone with the Wind* lamp," one globe above another. I wondered briefly if the clusters of hand-painted pansies were a subtle homage to Scarlett O'Hara's original name. A forty-watt bulb in a smoked globe makes reading in bed impossible . . . even more a problem than the little people's chifforobe. Ernie was beginning to mutter again.

Having super-sized ourselves from a double into a queen-sized bed decades ago, we spent a cramped and unhappy night rolling and tossing, trying not to slip into the abyss on either side of the bed.

In the morning, we staggered sleep-deprived down to our breakfast, too cold to manage more than a frosty nod to the "inn-mates," as we called the other guests.

The day proved glorious. We drove the Blue Ridge Parkway, marveled at the overlooks, roamed the streets of Asheville, visited Malaprop's Bookstore, ate healthily at the Laughing Seed, and eventually returned to our unheated TB retreat.

"I can't take it," Ernie said. "I'm going to find a nice, warm Econo Lodge with a TV. You're welcome to come." He flung his crumpled trousers over his shoulder and headed for the parking lot.

"I'm cutting my losses," he said, and drove off toward the highway.

He returned that evening looking refreshed and unwrinkled after his two-hour nap. We left to go eat supper at a lovely bistro on the side of the mountain. After he brought me home at ten-thirty and kissed me good-night, I headed to the Sourwood Suite alone.

He showed up the next morning for breakfast and picked me up. We rolled around the mountains for another day. Dropped off in late afternoon, I bathed, rested, dressed, and was fetched again for dinner, then returned to the inn. The inn-mates were giving us strange sidelong glances, but I was beginning to like our arrangement. I had not had a date in thirty-something years.

Will we go back to the mountains? Of course. Will we opt for a B&B? Not unless old age shrinks each of us by at least seventeen inches.

# Pruning Back

The recent rainy season gave the plants in our yard a rejuvenating shot in the limb; the green growth spurt is staggering. The shrubs all look as if they have returned from work as extras in that old Woody Allen film *Sleeper*, in which the vegetables grow to gargantuan size: cantaloupes the size of Oldsmobiles, broccoli two stories high.

Our bushes also seem to be on steroids, outsized and aggressively encroaching on the driveway and lawn. With clippers, I go out to do battle with the pittosporum, which I have always taken to be a rather staid, proper, Republican sort of bush. Ours now reaches skyward with the pretensions of a sequoia, obscuring the view of the road as you exit the drive. The yard looks much like a suburban jungle.

Our illeagnus is prone to long, unruly branches sprouting from its solid base. It definitely has a punk hairdo today. I like to give ours just a light trim, rather than a major haircut. No crew cut, just a little something around the eyes instead of a total facelift. I rip Virginia creeper and wild grapevines out of camellia bushes, shear the leafy tentacles over the drive, and decapitate a few nandina bushes to restore their long-lost feathery asymmetry.

Usually, my relationship to the yard is to walk through it on my way somewhere else or to sit out and enjoy the night air. It is rather like boating. I love to sit in the stern with a cool drink and enjoy the wonder of sailing. Do not expect me to unfurl the jib or wench in the spinnaker. Like sailing, yard work is strictly a spectator sport to me.

So why am I out here, clippers in hand, to wrestle nature to the mat? To beat my husband to the punch. He has an arsenal of weapons at his disposal for his attack on the unruly aspects of nature. He dons his pith helmet and ventures into the yard armed with a tool that looks like a scythe from a poster of Armageddon. The Grim Reaper never had a more formidable weapon. This gardening scythe is on a long pole with a pulley system that allows you to lop off branches waving ten feet above your head. You can saw leafy lateral branches into stubby extensions and restore a more acceptable shape to any tree or bush.

My husband is a disciple of the Male School of Pruning, having majored in geometric shapes. All plants must look like lollipops—some like giant Tootsie Pops, others like all-day suckers. A few triangles and trapezoids provide variations.

It may be a gender thing: the mathematical versus the naturalistic approach to life. Men focus on the control of nature; women are content to stand back and be amazed by it. Men dominate nature by wresting control of rivers by building dams, by imposing order on the ocean with jetties and sea walls. Women appreciate the surprise of where untamed nature may take them.

Under my husband's vigilant eye, our crape myrtles sport amputated limbs. They are nothing like the sprawling, anemic pink trees of my childhood, which, next to the mimosa and chinaberry, were the best to climb. Now severely pruned, they look as if they should join the stunted topiaries of Louis XIV's gardens.

My bifurcated dogwood, chosen for the two major trunks that promised future lateral limb splendor, lost the *bi* in its *bifurcated* one weekend when I went to Cary and returned to find my twin trunks surgically reduced to a tidy and more orderly single trunk.

I'm working on a new strategy. Strapping myself to a threatened yaupon or wax myrtle disappoints as an image of environmental martyrdom. But you have to start somewhere. Leave town and Ernie's path of destruction is wide. Think Chernobyl.

A recent trip to my daughter's bore out my gender theory of pruning. Her mailbox at the curb, a lush green Medusa of Carolina jasmine, reached monumental proportions. The mailbox and post, covered in the swirling, hairlike green vines, looked like a verdant refugee from the Woodstock era. My daughter loved it. My son-in-law was sharpening his clippers as I pulled out of the driveway and took one last, wistful look at the green Jimi Hendrix.

# *Perennials*

I'm inspecting the tiny plant in a paper cup I nurtured from Savannah to Wilmington last week. The woman from Keller's Flea Market said it was a Gadsden sunflower, the pride of Savannah, and would grow fifteen feet high with a bloom the size of a dinner plate. Looking dubiously at the little green shoot that resembles a bean sprout, I am overwhelmed yet again by the miracle of blooming things.

This little paper-cup plant transports me to first grade, when we cultivated carrot tops and sweet potato vines and butter beans in Dixie cups lined up at eye level on the window sill, checking daily for miraculous change. Like the connections we make with music—high-school proms, special first dates, and such—plants conjure up memories, too.

The banana shrub at our back deck, today full of lemony pistachio-shaped buds that do indeed have a heavy banana fragrance, plunges me into the 1970s, when we planted them around our patio in Mount Pleasant, South Carolina. The sweet aroma also transports me to a time when our children were young and so were we. Delighted that the plant could thrive in our new city, Wilmington, we purchased one on our very first visit to Orton Plantation. Our Indian hawthorn and camellias are also throwbacks to South Carolina days, when we planted the hardy species with spectacular results.

I've looked longingly at loquat trees at the arboretum plant sale and have decided we must add one to the yard. It will be a connection to junior-high days in the fifties. In Summerville, South Carolina, my family lived in the guesthouse on the grounds of the old Pine Forest Inn. The fascinating cottage looked like a Victorian wedding cake iced with white gingerbread trim. The sun porch, surrounded by giant loquat trees, was a round tur-reted space that Mama furnished with a daybed, old porch rock-ers, a table, a lamp, and boxes of *Life* magazines Daddy had collected every year since 1936. They were moved from house to house as we traveled across the South. The magazines, stored in open wooden crates, provided endless reading for rainy after-noons. Where else would I have seen the haunted eyes of British children transported on special trains from London during the blitzkrieg, or read the titillating story of the nine-year-old girl in Peru who had a baby? The subtropical loquats, heavy with orange globelike fruit, surrounded the sun porch, the site of many rev-elations on long-ago afternoons.

Daffodils catapult me back to the grove in front of Grandmother's house in Alabama, alive with yellow every spring, stretching as endlessly as Wordsworth's daffodils down to the road. A blanket of flamboyant double daffodils old folks called "scrambled eggs" and elegant jonquils with orange trumpets blan-keted the yard.

After Grandmother's death, the property was sold. The house was to be torn down. Friends who had long admired the abun-dance of March gold in front of the little Carpenter Gothic house came from town to dig the plants and take them home. Today, those daffodils are blooming all over Sumter County. At least I hope they are.

# The Big Potato Syndrome

From a newspaper article:

"Overstuffed kids: If you're going to make your kids clean their plates, don't put too much on them. 'Young children have a natural capacity to self regulate their food intake,' said Barbara J. Rolls, author of a Penn State study. 'But sometime between three and five years of age, they learn to ignore internal hunger signals and respond to other cues, including portion size.' "

This tidbit caught my eye because it targeted a recurring scenario in our family. All families have idiosyncrasies. Goodness knows, ours is no exception. But it is interesting when a repeated event becomes part of the family lexicon. And so it is with what we have dubbed "the Big Potato Syndrome."

It must have been back in the seventies when steakhouses sprang from the suburban soil like so many dandelions: Golden Corral, Quincy's, Western Sizzler, one or more in every town. The standard fare at these restaurants was beef: New York strip steaks, sirloin tips, ground steak, served with the ubiquitous baked potato with all the trimmings. For a bit more money, you could get a salad and stave off scurvy, but generally the meat and potato were it for the meal.

"This potato is entirely too big," my husband would always say when his plate arrived.

"It is huge, colossal. No one could eat such a big potato. It is almost obscene. It makes me lose my appetite," his lament would continue.

We all tried to ignore him, each of us dealing happily with his own obscenely large potato. But the monologue continued.

"Doesn't it make you lose your appetite?"

The children would roll their eyes and stare intently at their plates. No one answered. We all knew what was coming. A retelling of "the Depression Potato Story."

I heard the story in our early days of courtship, and it persists today. My husband swears that in his Goldsboro boyhood in the Depression, things were so tough and resources so limited in his household that the four children and his mother, widowed when Ernie was only four, had to split a cold Irish potato five ways for supper. Divided five ways—wrap your brain around that one. The story always gave me a logistical headache, since dividing one rounded potato five ways seemed a mathematical impossibility. Fractions never were my long suit.

My mother-in-law and I discussed the potato story not too long after Ernie and I were married. The truth was that, despite her widowhood and despite the Great Depression, the family was comfortable. There *was* no single potato to be divided beneath a dangling light bulb, as I envisioned the Van Gogh-like scene, but rather a bounty of hot vegetables, chicken, and biscuits at supper. I was the hapless victim of my husband's revisionist history. His version of the Great Depression centered around a metaphoric single potato.

Today, food servings have been super-sized and extra-valued. We're served oversized salads on serving platters, individual loaves of bread, tubs of pasta, mile-high desserts, and, of course, the big potato. I wonder why all of America isn't suffering from the Big Potato Syndrome. I'd discuss this with Ernie, but I'm afraid it would bring on another rash of Depression-era fiction.

# Squirrel Vendetta

There are two distinct groups of people in this world: squirrel lovers and squirrel haters. To some, squirrels are varmints; to others, the clown princes of the backyard. As with Madonna fans and detractors, it is love or hate. Indifference to the rascals is not an option.

These cheeky creatures claim the honor of being North Carolina's state mammal. State mammal? Who knew? We share in honoring the gray squirrel with Kentucky. Thirty-five other states have a state mammal, including the white-tailed deer, the beaver, and the whale. But a rodent? It's a tough sell.

I have a friend—she's my age, mind you—who has always said that if there is reincarnation, she's coming back as a squirrel. When pressed for specifics, she lists the stellar characteristics of being a squirrel: life in the great outdoors, a passion for frolic and play, expert escape skills (except for that occasional car), plentiful food supply, and a boundless capacity for sex . . . gymnastic sex at that.

My husband falls into the non-appreciative community when

it comes to squirrels. This despite the fact that, as an animal lover, he can watch four consecutive games of aquatic basketball played by non-conference dolphins at SeaWorld.

He is in charge of the bird feeder in view of our breakfast table and takes squirrel invasion personally. We currently have a repeat offender that has become amazingly adept at the leap between magnolia and feeder. We monitor his weight gain with astonishment. The squirrel is now the size of a Hyundai.

Promptly at six-thirty every morning, my husband cranks open the window, bams on the glass, shakes his fist, and shouts, "Get your blankety-blank out of my bird feeder!" The ex-Marine's expletives hang in the early-morning mist. I am glad our neighbors, whose bedroom is directly across from the window, are Quakers and not prone to violence.

We visit the Wild Bird Center to see about a shield we could put over the feeder to squirrel-proof it. We learn the shield is a Model T compared to the latest innovations. The saleslady tells us there are all sorts of new products aimed at deterring squirrels. As she gives us the spiel on each one, we nod gravely. The array is impressive . . . as are the prices. There is a long silence.

"But don't you have one that uses electricity? Something that would give them a little jolt to remember?" my husband asks.

The blood drains from the saleslady's face. She is visibly shaken.

"Well, there is one called the Wild Bill, but most of our customers don't want anything that draconian," she says. "But I think the Yankee Flipper will do the trick. It has a battery-operated circular perch beneath the feeder."

She invites us to watch a video of the Yankee Flipper in operation. The video will convince us of the sterling qualities of the Flipper, she tells us.

I don't know when I've seen better TV. The cardinals and finches come to the feeder, eat, and blithely fly away. Then the squirrel appears, jumps on the perch, and, because of his weight, is immediately hurled into space by the centrifugal force of the ingenious Flipper. Undaunted, he returns, only to be slung from the feeder again. The action is repeated. The squirrel is nothing if not persistent. After five minutes, the video is over. My husband refuses to leave. We watch three more times, then I drag him from the store to the car.

It is obvious to me that Santa Claus will pay an early visit to our house this year. I might even put out a saucer of assorted nuts and a Co-Cola by the fireplace for him.

# Courthouse Bay

We were there for only two years in the early sixties, but it remains an idyllic memory for us. Courthouse Bay, home for the Marine Corps School and the Second Assault Amphibian Battalion, is part of Camp Lejeune in North Carolina. It is a small, semi-independent village far removed from the main base, much like an island. Since it is located on the New River across from Sneads Ferry, trips for groceries and PX items meant a lengthy drive to "mainside," as we called it, reinforcing our island mentality.

The comfortable, two-story World War II houses had vintage maids' quarters attached, though no live-in help had been around for twenty-five years. Our shaded house backed up onto the New River, where an old-timey swing left by a former tenant swung out from a live oak to the bank's edge. A small marina just three houses down made a boat mandatory. We soon acquired a custom-made wooden craft constructed by an elderly boatbuilder in Sneads Ferry across the bridge. The old guy was not into frills, but the sturdy craft, all sixteen feet of it, was like a Chris-Craft to us. Boating across the river to Sneads Ferry to pick up fresh shrimp for supper and bubble gum for Howell became part of a regular father-son routine and a time-alone boon for pregnant me.

We met one of the most amazing women we have ever known while we were there. Betty Lou Jones from nearby Hampstead worked for us for two years at Courthouse Bay but became a friend for life. Betty Lou was a mix of optimism, hilarious anecdotes, and positive thinking. She arrived with her own poltergeist. Our cat Ralph was the first to notice. He began freaking out at the front-hall coat-closet door. He arched his tabby body into his most formidable stance and let out long, menacing growls at the closet door if it were the least bit open. Items moved mysteriously from closet to closet when Betty Lou was around—heating pad, umbrella, tennis shoes, jackets. And none of us was moving these things. We soon got used to it. A dozen poltergeists would have been a small price to pay for having Betty Lou in our lives.

Betty Lou's children all went to college. All are professionals; one is a lady dentist. Adored by her family as well as ours, Betty Lou was a mover and shaker in her community. She held an annual talent-show fund-raiser at her church, to which we were always invited. We piled into the crowded church for the Sunday-afternoon event. One by one, she called on members of the congregation to come up front and sing or recite a poem or dance. No one was exempt. At the close of the lengthy service, the collection plate was passed, and the grateful participants generously contributed and sang the closing hymn with enthusiasm. We were free for another year . . . another year to work on our presentations for the next talent show.

Though she had seven children of her own, Betty Lou was very proprietorial about ours. "We going to take our little fella for a walk now," she would say, my son's hand in hers. "Our baby is the most beautifulest there ever was," she always said to our infant daughter in her crib.

Even eight moves and twenty years later, we were in touch

with Betty Lou almost every month. She was one of only a dozen guests at my son's "family only" wedding. She sat next to the mother of the bride in the pew at the wedding of my daughter, Molly. Tears in her eyes, she whispered to me, "Our baby is the most beautifulest there ever was."

Back when our baby daughter arrived home at Courthouse Bay, we would sit by the river with our newborn in her German pram outfitted with a mosquito-net cover. Ralph the cat loved the addition to the family. He took to bringing offerings to the baby. Leaping, bloody bird in mouth, into the carriage, he dropped each trophy on the white mosquito net inches from Molly's face. Birds, a squirrel, a baby rabbit. Clearly, this could not go on.

Betty Lou offered to adopt the cat. We packed Ralph off to his new home in a cardboard box with the requisite air holes and a supply of food. Betty Lou's ride home to Hampstead, carpooling with five other workers from the base, made for a crowded commute, but we squeezed her in with the cat box. Somewhere past Holly Ridge, a yowling Ralph burst from the box. The driver slammed on the brakes, and the carpoolers bolted from the Volkswagen, scattering onto the shoulder of the highway. Ralph escaped into the underbrush. He was gone. A distraught Betty Lou gave a vivid report of the loss.

Twenty-six days later, we heard a noise at the back door. It was Ralph, the *Lassie Come Home* of Courthouse Bay. Twenty miles, four creek bridges, and one long bridge over the New River, and two pounds lighter . . . he was home. Betty Lou, first in the kitchen, opened the can of celebratory tuna.

# Deployment Déjà Vu

Newspaper photographs of the deployment of Marines from Camp Lejeune brought images back to me in a flood of memory. Women's arms flung around Marine husbands, toddlers looking up at their fathers' shaded faces, infants, unaware, pressed close against uniformed chests. The fierce commitment of these unknown families was as compelling as my own family photos. As the wife of a Marine in Vietnam, I understand what it takes to manage a life alone with small children during a controversial war.

In April 1965, my husband, three-year-old son, and six-month-old baby daughter were part of this same scene in a different war. Ernie, a career Marine, was off to Vietnam for thirteen months. Because families of deployed Marines were not allowed to remain on base, we packed our belongings and the children and moved from Camp Lejeune to Goldsboro for the separated tour of duty. Goldsboro is Ernie's hometown; his mother lived there; and the commissary, PX, and military hospital at Seymour Johnson Air Force Base would be available for the children and me. It seemed a good choice. I did not move in with Mamay, as we called his mother. I treasured our relationship too much to invade her house with our motley crew. We got a small bungalow not too far away.

The first weeks were busy with unpacking, sorting out the cousins and aunts in Ernie's family, and finding a church. After trying the downtown St. Stephens Episcopal, I opted for St. Francis Mission Church, a maverick choice, since the Borden cousins all went to St. Stephens.

The offbeat mission church suited me. Parishioners met each Sunday in an abandoned state prison farm, a whitewashed barracks building without any of the basic accouterments of church. Eventually, the mission lost its lease for the prison-camp facilities and moved to a bowling alley just outside the entrance of Seymour Johnson Air Force Base.

Every Sunday, vestrymen set up a portable altar in a bowling lane. The congregation, prayer books in hand, sat in folding chairs amidst gumball dispensers and silent, gaudy pinball machines. The bonus for the children: a gumball after the recessional. One friend cracked that St. Francis certainly couldn't be accused of having an edifice complex.

St. Francis eventually constructed a real church building. But never have services been as meaningful to me as those tucked into the lobby of the Goldsboro bowling alley among the garish machines. Support from this church family and from our actual kin was essential during those trying times.

Ernie sent reel-to-reel-tape letters from Vietnam telling how Marines were teaching local Vietnamese in Fu By to build pigpens so they could establish a ready meat supply for the village. He sent photos of the villagers and Marines working together on the pigpens. Ernie wrote of the need for a school building and supplies for the children of Fu By. He met an American plastic surgeon from Florida who was working in a nearby village with Vietnamese children who had been badly burned by napalm. The surgeon desperately needed a machine called a Brown Dermatome, which could make paper-thin slices of tissue from patients for grafting onto their burns.

A group of us from St. Francis, wanting to help, started an organization called RSVP—Reach the South Vietnamese People—and began collecting money for a Brown Dermatome and school necessities. It was something specific, something real we could do. The Associated Press picked up the local *Goldsboro News-Argus* story. Soon, contributions poured in—big checks, little checks, cash. We were elated. RSVP was able to buy two Brown Dermatomes, building materials for a school, notebooks, and pencils for the children of Fu By, children who had become as real to me as my own.

Recently, I found a roll of film in Ernie's old Marine Corps footlocker from Vietnam. Optimistically, I had it developed. Although the pictures are mottled from time, moisture, and heat, the miraculous images from almost forty years ago are riveting. Especially one grainy close-up of a solemn nine-year-old Vietnamese girl holding her toddler brother under a palm shelter, their wide eyes looking directly into the camera.

# The Blessing

I see them from time to time, people seated around restaurant tables, heads bowed, murmuring grace before they begin their meal, oblivious to other diners. Saying grace is still common in Southern towns, even at some pretty sophisticated restaurants. Frequently at private dinner parties, someone will say the blessing.

My granddaughter, Caroline, attended preschool at St. Paul's Episcopal Church in Cary, North Carolina, three days a week. She also went to Sunday school there. At age three and a half, she was very opinionated and had definite views on a host of topics, theology being a particular favorite of hers. Often from her car seat while I was driving, she launched into these pontifications.

She informed me on one trip downtown that she no longer wished to be called Caroline.

"What would you like for me to call you?" I asked.

She cocked her head and thought for a minute. "Something that begins with a G," she said slowly.

"Okay," I said. "What about Grace or Greta?"

"Nooooo. I think Goofy would be nice," she offered.

A long pause here.

"And I still don't want to be an Episcopalian anymore," she added. We had had this discussion before. She looked at me sideways.

I showed no reaction. I had weathered my own children's teen years and had mastered the impassive adult face mask. Never let them see you sweat.

"What would you rather be?" I asked in the most offhand voice I could muster.

"I'm going to be a Baptist."

I did not launch into the details of Jimmy Carter's dramatic, if temporary, falling away from his Baptist roots. I tried hard to remember she was only three.

"I don't want to talk anymore," she announced. "My mouth is tired."

I was sure I detected signs of Mama, gone these thirty years, alive and well in this funny little person.

At Thanksgiving, the extended family celebrated together. I was asked to say the blessing. Before I could even bow my head, Caroline launched into her school prayer:

Dear God, Thank you for this brand-new day,
Guide us as we learn and play.

We all commented on what a good job she had done, though Molly, my daughter, noted that Caroline sometimes said, "Guide us as we learn and *pay*," rather than "*play*." I guess it speaks to the economy.

A month later, the usuals gathered again for Christmas dinner, eight of us around the table. This time, Molly called on Caroline to say grace, since her Thanksgiving performance had let us know that her preemptive strike on the blessing would not give anybody else a shot at it anyway.

We bowed our heads and waited. Sure enough, the little voice was strong and clear. But it was not the usual brief couplet learned at school.

"Dear Lord," she began, "We thank you for the yummy food. We thank you for the big turkey and the sweet potatoes and the cranberries and the dressing and the broccoli and . . ."

I tried to stifle a laugh, but like those occasions when you get tickled in church, the harder I tried to swallow my laughter, the harder I snickered. Caroline, Baptist convert, undaunted, proceeded to bless every vegetable and pickle.

Next, she started on the family: "We thank you for Uncle Bob, Pop-pop, Nana, Aunt Nancy, Grandma . . ."

Her voice droned on and on, punctuated with long pauses as she decided where her next blessing would land. The gravy was beginning to congeal in the gravy boat.

Molly tapped the pray-er on the hand and said, "Thank you, Caroline, that will do nicely." We were ready to eat our cooled dinner. Every single one of us knew just how blessed we were.

# Before My Time

I continue to learn from my granddaughter, Caroline, on a regular basis. Some of our conversations are theological, some philosophical. At age three, she announced out of the blue that she wanted to convert from Episcopalian to Baptist. It turned out that this was a romance-based idea, rather than a real change in dogma. Her best friend in preschool, a fellow named Rob, was a Baptist. The denomination conversion and Rob both vanished by the time she turned four.

When Caroline was six years old and we were on the way to Chapel Hill, she asked if I knew where I was before I was born. I have difficulty remembering where I was yesterday, so I hadn't given my pre-birth location a great deal of thought. But apparently it was on Caroline's mind.

"Well," she went on assuredly, "I've been thinking a lot about it, and I know that I was up in heaven. I'm sure of that."

"And was God there, up in heaven?" I asked.

"Oh, yes, he has a very long beard. He's very nice."

I thought that Caroline's paternal image of God was going the traditional iconic path.

"He wears a long, bright orange robe with a rope tied around his waist," she said.

I wondered if she had spotted a Hare Krishna in the airport on her trip to Disney World.

"There was this big party going on in heaven."

I could tell she was warming up to her subject. "Were there any refreshments?"

"Of course." She seemed a bit exasperated at such an idiotic question. "It was a party. Cotton candy and a huge, big cake."

"A cake? Was it white or silver?"

"No, it was red, and it had writing on it that said, 'Praise Jesus.' "

I thought momentarily about the lasting influence of her friend Rob.

"Everybody was dancing and singing. We were all having lots of fun. But then I heard a voice in the lobby. 'Caroline Allred, calling Caroline Allred,' the voice called, so I had to go. It was time for me to be born."

We rode contentedly in silence for a while and pondered the revelation. I felt inadequate and sorry that I could not remember a pre-birthday party, but then Caroline was much closer in time to the experience than I.

All of this catapulted me back to conversations with my daughter, Molly, when she was just Caroline's age. One especially memorable one was about an assignment she had in first grade. The next day, she was supposed to stand up in front of her class and tell what her father did.

"What *does* Daddy do?"

I really didn't know the exact answer to that, but I said, "Well, he is a battalion commander in the Marine Corps."

I silently scrambled to be more specific. There was a long pause while we both thought about it.

"Gee," Molly said after a while, "I didn't even know he spoke battalion."

What a delight to have the second generation of these funny little girls and their take on theology and language.

# Searching for Pilgrims

Five-year-old Caroline telephoned us with exciting news. At school, she had learned about the Pilgrims and was full of stories of the first Thanksgiving. She had gotten the historic facts a bit mixed up with a story about a leper colony and ended up with some of the Pilgrims being sent off to an island to live by themselves with their terrible skin disease. But mostly she was on the right track. She knew about the *Mayflower* and Plymouth Rock and that the Pilgrims had come to America so they could have church the way they wanted to. "Don't forget to worship" was her parting shot to me as she relinquished the phone to my daughter.

Molly asked if I remembered the Pilgrim candles her grandmother Mamay had given us some thirty years ago. They were modest ornaments, from Hallmark, I think. Two five-inch wax candles with bland, waxy faces, one a Pilgrim woman in gray with a white apron and cap and the other a man in gray knickers and jacket with white stockings and buckles on his sturdy shoes. My daughter remembered the little candles vividly, as well as her grandmother telling the story of the first Thanksgiving as we set the decorations out each November. "Where are those candles now?" Molly asked.

I remember the candles very well. I recall unwrapping them about four moves ago after they had been stored in the attic. I was miffed that their wax bodies had been overcome by heat and their misshapen heads had melted onto their backs. They looked a bit like Quasimodos in Puritan gear. In an atypical move (I'm a card-carrying pack rat), I threw them out.

Now, in a wave of nostalgia, my daughter had linked her grandmother, who died in 1977, and the Thanksgiving story to those long-gone little wax figures. My own grandmama DNA kicked in, and I determined to find new Pilgrims for our Caroline that Thanksgiving, when the whole family would gather at our house to share a catered Roberts Market feast. (Mercy, I'm not so sentimental that I'm willing to whup up such a dinner on my own.)

It was a mission started too late. Pilgrims had sat unpurchased on the shelves for years, the store clerks told me, but now they were a hot ticket. Like green bean casserole and molded salads, they were back. But only paper plates and paper turkeys remained in stock . . . and pumpkins. I was beginning to think Pilgrims had become extinct.

I did find one cookie jar, a stout lady Pilgrim holding a cornucopia of fruit, but her benevolent chipmunk face reminded me of the balloons in the Macy's parade. It was not the look I was after. She would make an unfortunate centerpiece.

At one store, I spotted a dozen small turkey-shaped tea lights, but I couldn't figure out how to use them unless I surrounded the real turkey with the tiny turkey candles and lit them. That notion seemed a bit redundant, as well as a fire hazard, so I passed.

Little salt-and-pepper snowmen dressed in Pilgrim outfits were a bit too creative, I thought. In past years, I'd seen turkeys in Puritan garb toting muskets, which always struck me as something from the theater of the absurd.

I settled for eight three-inch ceramic place-card holders. A Pilgrim woman, a Pilgrim man, a Native American, and a turkey in a Pilgrim hat—two of each. Alas, they appeared to be victims of a mugger's stickup, since all of the ceramic figures had their tiny arms—or wings—raised high above their heads. That's how their little ceramic hands held the place cards up. It was a bit startling at first, like a flashback of Bonnie and Clyde in the bank, but perhaps right for our times.

As soon as Thanksgiving dinner is over, Caroline and I are going to talk about Pilgrims again . . . and maybe lepers.

# The Babysitter

Back when our children were young and my husband and I could no longer stand the bliss of parental domesticity, we turned to that most necessary modern convenience, the babysitter. In those olden days, the requirements were few and simple:

1.  A babysitter should be able to lift the receiver of the phone and dial for help if the situation demanded it

2.  She should show up at the designated time

3.  She should not drool noticeably

Naive souls that we were, we assumed the babysitters would play with our children, keep them from harm, and go home deliriously happy with their hard-earned fifty cents an hour.

It's all different today. For starters, my granddaughter did not allow us to use the word *babysitter*. Even at age four, Caroline found the title demeaning and insisted we call her caregivers by the euphemism *special friends*. It seemed to take the sting out of being left with an alien teenager.

Caroline's favorite special friend I found troubling. Her name was Astrid, and she lived several blocks away. Astrid was sixteen and looked like a Barbie doll on steroids. She was a good six feet tall without her wedgie platforms, her mass of Pre-Raphaelite curls held at bay by a dayglow scrunchie. I never saw Astrid in clothes where the top met the bottom. Naval exposure was her paramount fashion statement. She had an endless supply of Britney costumes worn even in twenty-degree weather, her midriff covered with goose bumps.

My daughter had to ask her not to wear the tank tops with risqué aphorisms stamped on them, since Caroline always tried to sound out the words and demanded explanations. The tank tops mainly involving the word *suck* and rhyming words. The rather large tattoo on the small of Astrid's back—which appeared to be a compass, interestingly enough—was ever exposed. I always thought it a shame the direction finder was not where Astrid had access to it.

A conversation with Astrid was tough going, despite the fact that I am generally at ease with teenagers, since I am in the classroom with them on a daily basis. This babysitter tended to look over your head vacantly with a distant, lobotomized stare while she pondered an answer to your question—even if the question was "Where do you go to school, Astrid?" I wondered if I had her name right but soon realized this slo-mo response was her modus operandi.

Caroline thought Astrid was fabulous. She loved that Astrid was so wonderfully tall. She studied the compass intently and asked Astrid to recount the tattoo experience yet again, as if it were a retelling of a favorite fairy tale.

Astrid was the favorite special friend for months, but even my daughter began to have concerns. The kitchen and den were always a monsoon aftermath when Astrid exited. Light housekeeping—even cleaning up the mess she and Caroline had made a few hours earlier—was not covered by the paltry five dollars per hour she got. The tattoo saga was wearing thin.

The last straw finally broke. My daughter called to tell me that Astrid would no longer be babysitting. On her last job, she had bundled Caroline up to return to her own house down the street. The adventure? A hair makeover. Astrid had to touch up her roots for her big date that night and was short on time. She provided Caroline with a running instructional commentary on the procedure. Caroline took it all in, as she did every move her idol made. On returning home, she repeated the wondrous preparations for the "hot date" step by step to her mother. The hunt was then on for a new special friend.

Somehow, I hoped her name would be Jane or Betsy.

# *Bloodlines*

It was logical, in a way. Both Japanese and Southerners revere family, have a certain choreography of social interaction, and regard good manners as the oxygen of society. So Caroline's fascination with all things Asian did not seem unusual at first. At two, my granddaughter adopted my Chinese doll Ling Ling as her own. At three, she was a devotee of sushi. Her best friend in kindergarten was Myumi. Japanese tea ceremonies were her passion.

When she was seven, Caroline's interest turned to genetic matters. She had already checked with her other Southern Scots-Irish-English grandma and had come up empty. Now, it was my turn.

"Are you sure we don't have any Japanese blood in the family, Nana?" the voice came long distance from Cary.

"I am sure," I said. "I'm really sorry, sweet pea. We only can manage Scots-Irish with a soupçon of German thrown in."

"None?"

"Nope. Not a drop."

A long, thoughtful pause.

"Then how about mermaid?"

"Not that I know of," I answered solemnly, thinking to myself that mermaid blood was more likely than Asian.

There was a long, disappointed sigh from the other end.

"Well, okay, then. I hafta go now, Nana."

On Sunday, the minister announced that after the service, the Kairos Prison Ministry was making a large poster with parishoner greetings to the inmates on it. Caroline wanted to send a message to the prisoners. The large poster already had a dozen notes on it.

"Let's read what some of the other parishioners have written. You read them, Caroline," said her mother.

" 'God is Love,' " she read aloud. "Here's another: 'Our prayers are with you.' "

"What are you going to write?" her mother asked, handing her the magic marker.

"I'm gonna write, 'Make better choices next time,' " Caroline said, as she began her greeting without a moment's hesitation.

I had to laugh when I heard the story. No Japanese or mermaid blood there. No theological abstracts or soft-pedaled sentiment or Zen philosophy. Nope. Only pure-o-tee Scots-Irish Presbyterian blood could come up with that message.

# The Girls

Like many couples who do not have children, my son, Howell, and his wife, Debbie, treat their dogs like four-legged offspring. Howell calls them "the girls" and regales us with stories about our grand-dogs' antics. Debbie's daddy refers to the two dogs as "the livestock."

Picture two yellow Labrador retrievers, the size of miniature Shetland ponies, named Bella and Cody. It is well that they are companion pets. Hauling these mega-dogs into a boat on a serious duck hunt would swamp any vessel under twenty-five feet.

Cody is a purebred lab and Bella is supposed to be, but we have our doubts. Bella looks very like a junkyard dog in the right light, and her behavior falls short of her supposed pedigree. She is definitely the smarter of the two. In demeanor, Bella is a canine Courtney Love to Cody's aging Grace Kelly.

The girls have never been in a kennel, so Nana babysits them when the need arises. The girls are entirely too delicate to go to a public kennel with hoi polloi, though we suspect Bella would take to it like a good ole boy to a tractor pull. The girls must remain in their own comfy digs, so I am the designated babysitter. "Grandma's coming to see you, girls!" Howell will whisper excitedly to the grand-dogs, whipping them into a frenzy of anticipation. My frenzy is less joyous.

One babysitting weekend, I carefully pushed my blood pressure medicines and assorted vitamins to the back of the kitchen counter to be sure they were in sight but safely out of the way. The pills were in one of those blue plastic seven-day medicine containers with individual lids. After feeding the girls, I got my jacket to take them out for the requisite tennis-ball-throwing session that Cody loves and Bella hates. Bella's indifference to retrieving reinforces my doubts about her origins, but she does enjoy beating Cody to the ball and playing keep-away, a throwback to the original dog in the manger.

I spotted a suspicious white pill dangling from Bella's lower lip, hurried to the kitchen, and found the pill container missing. Bella the contortionist was the culprit. By now, Cody was wolfing something from the pillbox on the living-room floor. Half a week's worth of pills were gone. I telephoned poison control. "Watch for symptoms," they said, "especially drowsiness." I frantically called my husband. He thought we should get going immediately. We would never be able to hoist the dead weight of the unconscious dogs into the car to get them to the vet if they passed out, he reasoned. We tore off to the clinic before that awful possibility occurred.

The girls were fine. I was not. It was another story to add to our canine repertoire.

In granddaughter Caroline's preschool, the children watched the Disney film *Lady and the Tramp* and ate a spaghetti lunch. After lunch, each child made a wish, which the teacher wrote on a paper star to hang on the bulletin board.

Sally said, "I wish for a bike with training wheels," which the teacher dutifully recorded on a star and affixed to the board.

Sam said, "I wish I had a puppy." He smiled, knowing he had trumped the bicycle. The teacher wrote down his wish.

It was Caroline's turn. She didn't hesitate.

"I wish my mommy had a tattoo," she said.

It is hard to explain to Howell that a Caroline story will always trump a story about "the girls." If they could only talk, it might be a more level playing field.

# Tidy

I try to get to see Tidy, my first cousin once removed, every summer when I go back to Alabama. It has become a pilgrimage. My cousin is the last of her generation and has no children, only a faithful niece, Anne, who visits her daily in the Greensboro Nursing Home. There, residents both black and white reside peacefully in a Southern version of God's waiting room in the self-proclaimed Alabama Catfish Capital. (There are several catfish capitals, but the granddaddy, or big fish, of them all is in Mississippi, which boasts the annual World Catfish Festival, complete with Catfish Queen and runner-up and hoards of decorated plexiglass catfish parading on their fins along the streets. In Alabama, they just paint a catfish on the water tank and call it a day.)

My cousin's name is Thyra Muckle—the *Thyra* for some long-forgotten Danish princess—but she is always called "Tidy." She will soon celebrate her 103rd birthday, and her age seems to be one of the few facts locked securely in her memory. She remembers, sometimes, the magnolia tree she and her sister Nora used to jump over in the front yard of the Muckle House, which is now a lovely bed-and-breakfast. Today, the magnolia towers well over two stories high.

Tidy has been in the nursing home for some time now. In the early years there in her late eighties, she dutifully attended all activities: singing Girl Scouts in uniform, Wendell's magic show (he's Lottie Sue's grandson), First Baptist's study of Corinthians, a clogging exhibition by a traveling group called Southern Shoes. But at age ninety-eight, she refused to go to the activity room one Wednesday to watch Loreen Spivey's macramé demonstration, which included instruction on how to make a shoe rack for your closet door. Tidy just refused to go. Not sick. Just refused to participate. Tidy never was much of a joiner. She crawled into her bed and wouldn't budge. No one could convince her to get up. Tidy always had spunk. But the officials of the home, like Lou Grant on *The Mary Tyler Moore Show*, hated spunk. They cajoled and threatened Tidy until she wore them down. They have long since abandoned any attempt to make her mobile. She hasn't gotten up since.

I remember Tidy from when she was younger than I am now, laughing with her sister Nora and Mama over some wildly funny story during summer visits. Tidy sent my grade-school children the most wonderful collection of Easter eggs, all made from real eggs with the yokes blown out—families of fish, pigs, sheep, cats, rabbits, and all manner of animals, a Noah's Ark of meticulously painted eggs. Nursery-rhyme and fairy-tale characters like Humpty Dumpty and Rapunzel joined the barnyard animals in an eggstravaganza of eggdom. My children were enchanted, and so was I. It became an Easter tradition to set them out, until one disastrous move to another town when the box disappeared. I like to think some other family sets those eggs out each spring and thanks the lucky day when the Mayflower box mysteriously appeared alongside their newly moved belongings.

Sometimes, Tidy remembers Mama. "You are almost as funny as your mama," she declared one visit. Tidy doesn't remember the Easter eggs. She lies in the bed as she has for the past five years, lounging grandly on her pillows, a Cleopatra on her barge (which seems consistent with her imperious decision about the macramé), smiling serenely at all visitors.

Thanks to the hairdresser who visits weekly to glamorize the lady residents, Tidy's hair floats like a silver nimbus around her head. She looks quite beatific, as if she has already sighted the pearly gates through the mists and, propped up, is ready to greet that final guest.

# The House That Isn't There

In hot weather, I *always* go back there, a mental trip to the place that meant summer to me. My grandmother's house in Alabama. Numerous cousins and aunts and uncles came and went during the hot months, but when I revisit the place in my mind, the house itself becomes a character as real as any I remember.

It was not an imposing house, but it did sit far back from the road with a long circular drive through what we called "the grove." In the spring, the circle was a yellow sea filled with Wordsworthian daffodils that brought to mind the line, "Ten thousand saw I at a glance." The simple, white Carpenter Gothic house, circa 1840, was typical of thousands dotting the Southern countryside. It sat on a rise that gave it a grand elevation over the twenty-five acres of pasture spread on either side of the yard, a setting far beyond the unpretentious architecture.

In summer, the mock-orange hedges toward the pasture burst with their knobby fruit—thick, heavy, leathery, inedible lime-colored globes. It was perfect ammunition for splendid fights among the cousins, an aggressive sport that left all of us children bruised and docile by dinnertime. Playing among the roots of the oak trees bordering the groove, we found colossal grasshoppers as long and thick as a roll of LifeSavers, with bold yellow and black markings. We sometimes tied thread to their large back legs and pretended we were taking the oversized insects for a stroll. They retaliated by staining our fingers with brown "chewing tobacco" liquid. Or we would race them against June bugs before releasing them back into the wild. I have never seen such gargantuan grasshoppers since.

The front gallery (we never called it a porch) stretched across the face of the house. Deserted by adults during the hot midday hours, the gallery's rockers, gliders, and swing were by late afternoon and evening populated by both adults and children, talking, rocking, and swinging to create some small breeze to stir the heat, ice tinkling faintly in tall glasses of lemonade or tea. The faint hint of talcum powder mixed with that of newly cut grass in the pasture.

The parlor was a light, airy space with windows that went all the way to the floor in another vain architectural effort to capture a breeze. It never was "the living room," for no one lived there; we children rarely entered the sacred space except to get books from the floor-to-ceiling bookcases that lined the entire back wall of the room. The heavily starched muslin curtains were perfectly drawn back, sweeping the floor, another hint that the room was seldom used.

The utilitarian dining room had an oversized table, the inevitable bookshelves that were in every room in the house, and two sideboards whose marble surfaces held bowls of the fruit du jour—peaches, plums, persimmons, figs, whatever was in season. A tin of Betty's tea biscuits was always there, too, a sort of thick shortbread cookie with a faint almond flavor, perfect with a cold drink.

The kitchen, once a separate cookhouse, had been moved to connect to the back gallery, which, like its sister up front, stretched the width of the house. At one end, two iron beds behind a lattice screen served as a makeshift sleeping porch for overflow children. At the other end of the gallery, pie safes with screen doors and primitive wood latches to secure the shelves of jellies, sugar, and staples stood on either side of the kitchen door. An enormous black wood stove squatted in the middle of the kitchen, a room always heavy with the smell of bacon and cornbread and fried chicken, even when no meal was being prepared there. A permanent perfume was in its floorboards.

I remember the summer coolness inside the house, and the sounds. The whine of cicadas and spring peepers drifted through open windows in the evening; oscillating fans whirred in every room; the Victrola crackled in the back hall when someone played the old Caruso records; the train's long, lonely moan came across the pasture as it rattled south to New Orleans. In reality, the un-air-conditioned house could not have been cool. An oven full of children, it could not have held that wondrous quiet I remember so vividly.

Now, there's a subdivision named Shady Heights on the hill where Grandmother's house stood. Brick split-levels and two-story clapboard houses crouch under the oaks in the grove. The mock oranges are gone.

But every summer, I still go back to that white Carpenter Gothic house, its swings and gliders swaying gently on the long front gallery in the heat.

# The Hanging of the Greens

It is an ancient custom, this hanging of the greens, harking back to the Druids in the British Isles. Every December, Christian churches all over our country have ceremonies, services, or suppers to "hang the greens." It is the season to bring inside fragrant evergreen boughs of holly, cedar, pine, spruce, and fir, symbols of life eternal and the living spirit of God, to decorate the churches for Advent and the Christmas season.

The greens service at the Church of the Servant Episcopal Church combines the lifting of an enormous garland of boxwood around the circle of the sanctuary with a unique reenactment of the Nativity. A family service, the pageant involves all the parishioners, especially the little ones. Children of every age are there in costume.

The costumed youngsters are not limited to the mundane sheep, goats, cows, and other stable dwellers one usually expects, though there are a few barnyard creatures. More exotic animals and storybook characters also appear. Along with the child-beasts, a real poodle with a tinsel halo and a pair of Chihuahuas are regulars at the service, accompanied by an elderly golden retriever with angel wings. All come to be a part of the miracle-in-the-manger scene.

The pageant starts with the Annunciation to Mary. Lurching in to announce the news is the tallest Gabriel imaginable, complete with an impressive set of wings at least five feet tall (seemingly gray cement, but actually poly-Styrofoam), courtesy of the Screen Gems film studios. We always startle at the entrance of this imposing figure. Some little ones even cry.

This play has two live Marys. The first, a pregnant parishioner, represents Mary before the birth of Jesus and is, at the proper time, replaced by an unpregnant Mary. After the first Mary exits, the nonpregnant parishioner playing Mary after the birth sits in front of a manger with a live parishioner baby and Joseph, who, mercifully, retains his role for the whole show.

(One year, the pregnant first Mary, led around the center circle by her tall Joseph looking for a room at the inn, had an unscripted attendant. The Mary's own two-year-old toddler, attired in angel wings, clutched the corner of her mother's blue robe and trailed three feet behind the holy couple, like a tiny pilotfish following Mama.)

The children of the church are invited to the altar and manger, where the living tableau of the real infant, the nonpregnant Mary, and Joseph wait. As the priest reads from Saint Luke, youngsters wander up in pairs or singly to see the holy family. Then the children sit on the floor in front of the manger. They are a spectacular assemblage. Some are in traditional shepherd, Wise Men, or animal garb. But most come in an anachronistic variety that is dazzling: ballerinas, Spider-Man, a possum, and one small child with a brown paper bag over his head with black crayon marks on the front (we took him to be an owl). At least two Barbies and/or princesses attend and, one year, a giant strawberry. All gather at the manger. They may not be the traditional visitors from that holy night long ago, but the look of wonder on each child's face is unmistakable.

*153*

When the large cardboard box is brought to the front, a child is selected to unwrap each crèche figure and place it in the stable. The explanation of every papier-mâché character follows.

Finally, the real Santa Claus—not in the jolly red elf costume, but in the regal crimson velvet robes of the bishop of Myra, complete with miter and crosier—arrives with a bag of small gifts for each little Barbie, owl, and strawberry. In the glow of candlelight and the fragrance of greens, we sing one last carol. The season is upon us, and our hearts are filled with "comfort and joy."

*Part III*
*Otheren*

# Celebrity Sightings

Harold Brodsky says the cult of personal fame emerged in its modern form in the frenzy that surrounded Sarah Bernhardt at the turn of the twentieth century. The Divine Sarah had a following on both sides of the Atlantic. Wildly popular, the eccentric actress died in 1923. A quarter-million grieving Parisians paid their respects, filing by her casket, which she had taken to sleeping in long before her final rest. Her popularity was remarkable, considering it was decades before media coverage assailed us from every direction.

My mama always said she had only one desire to fraternize with the famous. Her fantasy, cherished from her girlhood in the Roaring Twenties to the day she died, went like this: Mama is on the dance floor in her red brocade flapper dress (the one with the fur trim and gold mesh godets in the skirt) when her dancing partner turns toward a stranger, who taps on his shoulder, and asks to cut in. Her dancing partner relinquishes her hand to the new partner. Mama realizes it is Fred Astaire as the two of them whirl away across the dance floor. I always loved her fantasy. It was so Twenties.

I've had my own Forrest Gump moments when I have brushed elbows with the famous. I have been a groupie of one sort or another for years. During my college days at Chapel Hill, I saw and shook hands with Carl Sandburg, Robert Frost, and Louis "Satchmo" Armstrong at campus appearances. Also at Carolina, I met Eleanor Roosevelt at a tea at the president's house. Only about twelve students were there, so we had an opportunity to really talk with her, though I don't recall a thing that was said. In my home, she was not as beloved as FDR. My parents always called her "Eleanooore" (as FDR pronounced it) and thought her coal-mine activities unsuitable for any lady, much less a first lady. To me, she was a warm, grandmotherly type who was better looking in person than in photographs. Truth be told, I was not really impressed by this meeting with the great lady until twenty years later, when I had a little more sense.

I met Gloria Swanson, the tiniest slip of a woman, in New Orleans, and the affable Andy Griffith at the 1958 Azalea Festival, along with Queen Azalea Esther Williams, from whom I first heard the F word, in the ladies' room at the Lumina at Wrightsville Beach. I was on the reviewing stand at the Citadel in the 1970s when England's Prince Charles, still a bachelor, addressed the cadets and faculty. We were expecting a dolt and were surprised and charmed by the prince's self-deprecating wit . . . and his ears.

Tom Wolfe's *Bonfire of the Vanities* is one of my favorite novels. I met Wolfe at a small family wedding and was amazed at how few groupies seemed bold enough to go up to the literary lion. Then I realized most people there were kin. I circled him like a buzzard around road kill but did not approach him to talk. Eventually, the aging groupie gene kicked in, and I went over, introduced myself, and had a lengthy conversation about university life and the Introduction to Lit courses I was teaching at the University of North Carolina at Wilmington. Wolfe seemed genuinely interested in my classes and my take on university students. I read later that his next book, *I Am Charlotte Simmons*, would center on the higher-education system. He struck a camera pose for me in his cream-colored suit, the same pose I had seen in *Town & Country*. I snapped a picture of him, arms akimbo, one foot cocked, just like the photos you always see in *The New Yorker*. My Sure Shot camera couldn't do him justice. I needed a Leica. Tom Wolfe does not disappoint.

Another who lives up to his billing is author Pat Conroy. We chatted at length in Raleigh at a book signing shortly after his unflattering novel about the Citadel, *The Lords of Discipline*, was published. I bought his book as a Christmas present for my husband, Ernie. Conroy and I laughed over Citadel stories; my husband had been there as provost marshal, and Conroy remembered him. The author went on and on about Southern women in general and his own mama in particular. He autographed my copy of his novel. It was not until I got home that I read what he had written: "To Ernie, An officer and a gentleman . . . who has great taste in women." The blarney of that Irish Southerner. Talk about not disappointing!

# The Blurb

Southern mamas are a very special breed, much written about, the objects of unflagging devotion, particularly among Southern men. This Southern mama story reveals a couple of her strengths: shrewdness and a keen understanding of the nature of teenagers. It is not about my own mother but about my mother-in-law. I told the story to Pat Conroy in 1980, and he loved it so much that he threatened to steal it. A good twenty-something years later, I wrote him and reminded him of the story. As a result, he gave me a blurb for my new book. I knew a bona fide Southern boy couldn't resist a quintessential mama story.

Here is the letter: .

Dear Mr. Conroy,

I met you in Raleigh years ago when your book about the Citadel, *The Lords of Discipline*, came out, so that gives you some idea of the time lapse. My husband, Ernie, was the provost marshal at the Citadel from 1970 to 1980, and you were kind enough to inscribe the book for him. It was the perfect Christmas gift.

I know you don't remember me, but you might remember the story I told you about Ernie going off to the Citadel at the young age of sixteen. His Presbyterian widowed mother—her children all called her Mamay—drove him to the Citadel and helped him unpack in his barracks room. She made him promise to read a chapter from the Bible every night. She placed her Bible on his nightstand.

Ernie began his year at the Citadel with his five-dollar-per-month allowance—the widow's mite—which had to cover laundry, notebooks, and sundry other needs. The year was tough in many ways, and being financially strapped made it even more difficult. Ernie didn't even have money for a movie or dinner out at Henry's in downtown Charleston.

At the end of the school year, Mrs. Graham arrived at the Citadel to fetch Ernie's things and take him back to Goldsboro. As they were gathering his belongings, she picked up the Bible on his night table and asked him, "Son, did you keep your promise to read a chapter from the Scriptures every night?"

"Of course, Mamay," he assured her, folding the last shirt into his suitcase. "Every single night."

She flipped open the Bible to Genesis, removed the crisp twenty-dollar bill tucked into the crease of the page, opened her change purse, deposited the bill, snapped it shut, turned, and headed for the door with a box of his clothes.

Neither mother nor son said another word or ever mentioned the incident. You can rest assured that the lesson was one of the most valuable Ernie learned at the Citadel.

I know you are a softie where Southern women are

concerned, so I hope I can leverage that weakness (or strength?) into a comment from you about my book. I am going into a second printing of *Turn South at the Next Magnolia* on the first of next month. Thank you so much for your consideration.

Sincerely,
Nan Graham

I got a phone call from Mr. Conroy forty-eight hours after I mailed the letter and book. He said, "You got me. How could I possibly refuse a letter like that?" He would be most happy to give me a blurb for the book. Every good Southern boy is a push-over for a mama story. Down South, every day is Mother's Day.

# A Fishy Story

My son has told me this story several times, and it is a good one. It happened at the Cape Fear Blue Marlin Tournament at Wrightsville Beach several years ago on board the *Margueritaville*. Four or five of my son's friends had entered the contest in pursuit of the big fish and the big money—twenty thousand dollars. The crew pooled their resources for the entry money and loaded supplies aboard the *Margueritaville*. The guys were confident that this was their lucky day. Miles out on the ocean, sun blazing, they were catching fish, but not the elusive giant marlin that would bring them the big bucks. As the day wore on, so did the spirits of the crew, whose optimism grew as thin as their tempers.

Finally, in the late afternoon, Robert got the big strike. It was a huge fish, all right, and a fighter at that. After a Hemingwayesque struggle, the beast was pulled in. A good forty-eight-pounder, a real whopper. Trouble was, it was not a marlin. But it was one of the biggest tunas any of them had ever seen.

It was getting time for the crew to head back. They didn't

talk much over the roar of the engine. There wasn't much to say. Despite the big catch, the day was a bust as far as the tournament and the prize money were concerned.

Back on land, they decided to make the best of the situation and have a tuna cookout to end all such dinners. They headed to one of the guys' houses to prepare the meal. Well, the dinner was memorable, a tuna bonanza with slaw, hush puppies, all the trimmings, and unlimited beer. There was so much tuna that the crew sliced the remaining meat into generous slabs and put them in large Ziploc bags. Each guy took an armload of fish to deal out to lucky friends and neighbors. We were on the recipient list. The tuna was out of this world when we grilled it the next night.

The crew found out the very next day that no winning marlin was caught in the tournament. In fact, no marlin was caught at all. So by default, the committee declared that the prize money would go to the biggest fish of any species caught. The largest entry for the prize money so far weighed in at forty pounds—a good eight pounds lighter than the *Margueritaville*'s giant tuna. But the tuna was gone—cleaned, cut up, grilled, frozen, dispersed, and devoured across New Hanover County. It was surely one of the most costly meals on record.

And now, the rest of the story, as Paul Harvey intones. I called Robert Edgar, captain of the *Margueritaville*, in Rhode Island to get the particulars, and guess what? This wasn't the story at all. There were two tournaments. The crew members actually won the first-prize purse in one of them. In the other, they did catch a giant tuna but didn't bother to submit it in its category. The prize was meager, so they opted for dividing up and eating most of the fish and giving away what they couldn't consume.

That's it. There was no story. It was exactly what it appeared to be, a fish story with an O. Henry finale.

# Camp Wannadroppawawa

We've had an interesting Memorial Day weekend—one without a single drop of running water. Our pump is on the fritz. After sixteen years of dependable service, we really can't complain. But I do. I remember drinking icy well water from a gourd dipper on several occasions as a child. But this is now, and water is supposed to come out of a faucet.

We were annexed into the city three and a half years ago. We pay city taxes. But we have yet to see a drop of city water, despite the fact that our street hardly qualifies as rural and city water pipes run within eight houses of ours. But that is another matter. I won't burden you with my municipal diatribe.

Our deep-water well pump shut down without warning on the rainy Friday before the holiday. Something about a collapsed line. After a long session with the plumber and another pump failure, my husband, Ernie, clad in his yellow nor'easter, went into full testosterone mode. He and the plumber slogged through puddles in the downpour trying to solve the pump problem, without success.

That was days ago. I am trying to be a good sport, but as the primitive living drags on, my sportsmanship is wearing thin. I am on a journey of self-discovery and am finding out things I wish I didn't know. I realize that I belong to the school of obsessive-compulsive hand washing. This is difficult to sustain when I have to pour bottled drinking water over my hands, soap, lather, pour again, then rinse. It's a lot of water and a lot of trouble, multiplied many times a day. Who knew I was really Howard Hughes in drag? Minus the toenails, of course.

Ernie is on full red alert. He has not been this focused since the Iraqi war began, when he refused to leave his bunker until the statue of Saddam was toppled on TV. I have heard too many times now the story about how his unit spent seventy-six days bathing out of their helmets in Vietnam. I refuse to bathe out of a helmet. I don't even have a helmet.

The hose from the shallow-well pump in the garden now goes through the window into our master bath, in which three buckets sit. (We went shopping at Wal-Mart and returned with a trousseau of four buckets of varying styles and shapes.) One bucket is positioned by the toilet, ready for a tank refill. Another stands full on the sink top, ready for compulsive hand-washers. The most elegant bucket, a burnished platinum number, waits in the power room for the arrival of unsuspecting guests, who may wonder if they're auditioning for the next season of *Survivor*.

The remaining bucket of water acts as a kitchen sink. Now that the rain has stopped, Ernie, clad in Bwana Bob outfit (safari khakis and pith helmet), boils water with great gusto to wash our few dishes. He seems unusually animated in these activities. I suspect that his dormant camping/bivouac gene has kicked in. I do not carry that particular gene.

We invested in paper plates and cups and plastic utensils for the duration, but he persists in using a few dishes every day, so he can boil water and wear his pith helmet. Ernie is in his element, while I have turned into a whining old lady, trapped here at Camp Wannadroppawawa. I'm not a happy camper.

They say that adversity reveals a person's true character. I am *so* hoping that is not true.

# A Very Civil War

They are awakened about dawn for the big day. The two live very different lives, perhaps reflecting the side of the Mason-Dixon on which each lives. The difference in lifestyles is apparent right off the bat.

Phil is unceremoniously removed from his Spartan living quarters in the town library in Pennsylvania to ride out to Gobbler's Point and is placed in a burrow leading to a faux tree stump. He then emerges out of the faux stump to the snapping cameras of the paparazzi for his televised weather prediction and returns to his solitary library digs to wait out another year.

Beauregard arises to reveille sounded by a professional bugler and saunters out on the veranda of his Georgia antebellum mansion, complete with white columns. A bronze marker proclaims the mansion's name: Weathering Heights. A sundial adorns the lawn; Beauregard is something of a Luddite. His mansion is reputed to feature a wine cellar, but word is the cellar is really a large hole for burrowing. He lives large in a setting befitting a Georgia groundhog with social pretensions. Groundhog Day events at the Yellow Ranch include a local celebrity bell-ringing, after which Beauregard emerges from the veranda and either sees his shadow for six more weeks of winter or doesn't, which means spring is just around the corner. Either way, Beauregard noshes happily on sweet potato chips after the announced prediction and flashes his Southern smile for the camera.

Both celebrities are a bit on the "stout" side, as we say down South. Phil begins breakfast with an entrée of dog food and finishes with some strawberry ice cream. Beauregard, whom intimates called "Beau" and acquaintances call "the General," dines on fresh strawberries and peas these days, having recently become weight conscious. Threatened with an enforced Atkins regime if the pounds kept piling on, Beau was in imminent danger of being called "Bubba." One humiliating rumor had it that a carpenter was called in to widen the door on the Tara look-alike mansion to accommodate the more ample Beau's comings and goings.

Both woodchucks are weather prognosticators. One has a title and a full name and two doctorate degrees—a DWP (doctor of weather prognostication) from the University of Georgia and a doctorate in "Southern groundology" from Georgia State University. The other does not.

But there is no question who receives more ink. Punxsutawney Phil is nationally known, while Beau, perhaps with a delicacy that reflects his Southern upbringing, shies away from notoriety. Bill Murray's film *Goundhog Day* has garnered a cult following and assures Phil's continued fame. He is arguably the most famous woodchuck, or whistle-pig, in the world. Beau, on the other hand, is happy to be a local hero, to live the good life, and to receive commendations from the National Weather Service.

Phil in Punxsutawney, Pennsylvania, and General Beauregard Lee in Lilburn, Georgia, each work one day per year: February 2. But the difference in their performances is *huge*. Blame it on location, location, location. The sunny South *is* more likely to produce a shadow, so Beau may have an edge on predictions. Or the performances may indicate the genetic abilities of the groundhogs themselves.

In any case, the record is clear. Phil's weather accuracy is a sad 37 percent, while Beau's is a startling 93 percent. Guess we don't have to wonder who wins this war.

# Dutch

Our neighborhood doesn't have many children, so we have to rely on alternate trick-or-treaters . . . dogs. Years ago, a yellow Lab named Max used to appear at our door in clever costumes. One year, Max came in green surgical scrubs and an operating mask, a stethoscope dangling from his neck. He was Doggie Howser. Another Halloween, the yellow Lab wore an NFL jersey and was billed as the Wide Retriever. But Max stopped coming when his owners had their own real child.

My favorite canine trick-or-treater didn't come to our door 'this year. She belonged to our neighbor two doors down. Her name was Dutch, a most extraordinary chocolate Lab. She had all the traits Labs are famous for—she was smart, patient, loyal, whimsical, serene, companionable. Even our Westie, Annie, who tends to dislike other dogs, was such a Dutch fan that she would take off for a swing by Dutch's house whenever she was off the leash.

Dutch grew from rambunctious puppyhood (when she ate the kitchen baseboard and cabinets one afternoon and polished off the feast by consuming a hefty collection of three-by-four glossy photos from the counter) to a calm and amazing dog that always knew where her center was. Somehow, I imagined Dutch practicing yoga in her free time, sitting in the lotus position, humming her mantra—"Goood dooog, goood dooog"—under her breath.

Dutch made her Halloween debut in a minimalist costume that reflected her initial insecurity about her identity. She came to our door as a Dalmatian in a simple white T-shirt with large black dots in a random pattern. That was it. But her patient Labrador smile gave her away. Her costume was Dalmatian; her grin was pure Lab.

The next October, Dutch arrived as a rabbit, again showing a basic insecurity about her sense of self. But her more elaborate costume—a white shirt and large pink satin bunny ears—did show more attention to detail. We were prepared for her with dog-biscuit treats that Halloween.

By the next year, Dutch had found and "owned" her character. She appeared at the front door in full camouflage jacket sporting a haphazard variety of hash marks and chevrons. An authentic red beret at a jaunty angle completed the ensemble. Her self-confidence was unmistakable. I always suspected Dutch was a closet feminist.

The Halloweens rolled by. Dutch as a striped tabby cat. Another year, Dutch as an angel, complete with wings and halo. And my personal favorite, Dutch as a ballerina. The tutu was yellow net with white polka dots, accented by a yellow satin sash with a lace pouf atop Dutch's chocolate head. Unfortunately, the lace headpiece tended to slip and ended up a ruff for Dutch's furry neck wattle. The total look was less than Bolshoi.

Last year, Dutch returned to her earlier minimalist look and arrived almost au naturel. She was a Halloween ghost. Wearing only a thin coating of what appeared to be talcum powder, she stood patiently at the door awaiting her Halloween treat, looking a bit like a giant from-scratch biscuit. Her enormous eyes were sad and patient, but her tail wagged slowly in appreciation as she took the kibble and retreated in ghostly silence to her waiting owners at the end of the walkway.

Dutch's last costume proved prophetic. She has been gone some six months now. Last night, we didn't have a single trick-or-treat dog come to our door. Halloween just isn't the same these days.

# Fern Frenzy

Not much of a gardener, I never thought I would get caught up in ferns. The only fern I really know is the ubiquitous Boston fern, that showy domestic from Harris Teeter I invest in from time to time. Bostons really should consider using their real name, *Nephrolepsis exaltata*. It's so wonderfully pretentious.

Even with their lavish display of green, my Bostons go the way of all flesh . . . correction, the way of all fronds. I once even bought a kelly green air fern, which managed to die a slow and lingering death. The ferns indigenous to our backyard when we built our house were wiped out after a hurricane brought down trees and pounded the primordial plants into oblivion.

My fern opportunity came the day after I arrived in Alabama for my summer stint there. Dr. Richard Holland, president of the University of West Alabama and a botanist, was to be a judge at the Birmingham Fern Society's twenty-eighth annual Fern Show. He and his wife, Becky, invited me to go along to the Birmingham Botanical Garden, the elegant setting for the show and sale.

The pteridologists, or fern lovers, meet monthly at the botanical garden. They are fiercely dedicated to their stated mission: "To promote interest in hardy ferns and fern allies and maintain the Fern Glade within the Botanical Garden." I wondered vaguely who the fern allies could be. Would friends of ferns come to their defense if they were maligned or attacked? Would clovers and dandelions lock leaves or fronds and unite against an assailant? Do ferns have enemies?

I learned later that the fern allies are horsetails, quillworts, and club mosses, plants as ancient as ferns, dating back 400 million years. All are the basis of our coal formations today.

Posters at the botanical garden proclaimed the anticipated arrival of keynote speaker John Mickel of the New York Fern Society, the author of *Ferns for American Gardens*. The "internationally recognized fern expert" had the pteridologists fired up for the evening program. They chatted excitedly about the topic: "Hot New Ferns for American Gardens." The lecture sounded like a sizzler for fern fanatics, who were hardly the bloodless bunch I had anticipated. They were as giddy as rock groupies over the arrival of Bon Jovi. John Mickel was a hottie in the pteridology world. I was really sorry I wasn't going to be able to stay for the lecture. I envisioned a light show with pyrotechnics, skanky dancers, and rock music to accompany the presentation.

It took two and a half hours for the sixteen judges to name the winners amongst the ferns. As a layman, I found the array of contestants a sea of look-alikes. All seemed identical green clones to my untrained eye. But each winning frond in its clear beaker sported its blue ribbon as proudly as any orchid. Surprisingly, there was even a category for *Fern Impostors*. It turns out that the asparagus fern is really a lily posing . . . as a fern.

At one o'clock, the fern judging was over, the locked doors were thrown open, and the waiting crowd rushed in to view the winning fronds and buy the ferns on sale at the other end of the room.

Ah, the fern sale! I had not seen that kind of intensity in

Birkenstocks since Chapel Hill in the 1960s. Men and women in jeans, brogans, and shirts with environmental slogans stampeded to the *Southern Maidenhairs*, past the *Silver Cloak* and the *Alabama Lip* sections, grabbing little pots of *Blunt-Lobed Woodsia* and *Peacock Ferns*. *Purple Cliff-Brakes* and *Adder's Tongues* were jammed into children's red wagons and hauled to the checkout cashier.

The veteran shoppers, a hardy bunch, were accustomed to the melee, but I got caught in a near-fracas between two couples contending over one fabulous *Ebony Spleenwort*. I also witnessed a bit of ugly shoving in the *Bublet Bladder* and *Eared Lady* section. Who knew that fern shopping is a contact sport?

The fern names alone made my head spin. I paused by the *Fern Impostors* table and looked sympathetically at the last remaining asparagus fern. A fern that was really a lily at a fern show. I knew just how it felt.

# The End of the Affair

As the Greek philosopher Heraclitus wrote concerning time, change, and flowing water, "You cannot step twice in the same river." I accept the departure of the drachma as currency. I can stand the end of *Frasier* on TV. But the loss of my darling L. M. Boyd . . . that is a different thing.

I never really intended to go public with this secret, but since the relationship ended unexpectedly, I've decided to confess all . . . to you and to my husband. I have had this thing for L. M. Boyd for years now. I had no idea that our relationship was falling to pieces until I read about the break-up in, of all places, the newspaper.

On second thought, that *would* be the place I would find out about the end of this affair. L. M. Boyd's unsmiling, postage-stamp-sized picture with that heavy Fuller-brush mustache and those solemn eyes (perhaps a distant cousin of Joseph Stalin?) was practically the first thing I saw every single weekday morning in the *Wilmington Star-News* in his syndicated column, "Just

So You'll Know." He was as essential as my first cup of morning coffee. My daily fix from the trivia guru.

He knew me so well. Being an English-major type, I was easily addicted to his brand of trivia. My obsession for my dear L. M. Boyd had been going on for some fourteen years. You can imagine my amazement and pain when I read his final words to me that last Friday:

"That's it. Thanks. I'll miss you. But it's time to hang it up. Goodbye. L. M. B."

The dramatic December 30 farewell note was so like him. Terse. Pithy. Unexpected. Economical. To the point. Unapologetic. He always was something of a drama queen.

There were things I did not know about my secretive Mr. Boyd. He had an alias, for goodness' sake: Mike Mailway. It's just as well I didn't know that bit. The corny pseudonym might have cooled my ardor. Mike Mailway certainly lacks the *je ne sais quoi* of L. M. Boyd.

He had been unerringly faithful, or so I thought, until that moment when I read his farewell words. I could always count on him to feed my trivia appetite. Six days a week, week in, week out, year after year. Some 187,200 items over forty years, according to the *Star-News*.

Where else will I learn mysteries of nature such as the fact that you can hear banana plants grow, or that a dab of vinegar will relieve the pain of a jellyfish sting, or that butterflies and bats often sleep together?

Who will share necessary life lessons? Who will tell me that when a person's voice rises (according to experts), he is lying; or that because of tomb art, we know the Egyptians believed in sex after death; or that when you taste copper in your mouth, you are about to be struck by lightning; or that if you live in the Hague, your dog can ride the trolley on a child's ticket; or that adding two tablespoons of lemon to your rice will make it exceptionally white?

Who will confide vital historical secrets such as the fact that the well-known life of the party Calvin Coolidge carried his pet raccoon, Rebecca, around on his shoulder at the White House; or that in 1834, Charles Goodyear, jailed for bad debts, began his experiments to vulcanize rubber in his prison cell; or that in ancient Rome, there were no strictly female names, only feminized names such as Julia, Claudia, and Cornelia; or that the first elephant arrived in America in 1796?

One Wednesday, he whispered in my ear that F. Scott Fitzgerald always drank gin and called it "the writer's vice." Scott's friend, foe, and fellow boozer Hemingway referred to his favorite gin as "the giant killer." Faulkner's poison was also gin. Fitzgerald must have been right.

On Monday, I laughed when L. M. told me that a North Dakota wit named his newly mated yaks Yak and Yill. L. M. is such a card. From what L. M. calls his "Love and War File" came this quote from writer Adela St. John: "I learned there is little difference in husbands. You might as well keep the first." I am afraid this reveals L. M.'s fear of intimacy.

Now, it's over. Will I survive without all this essential information? Well, I have a few surprises of my own, L. M. What I haven't told you is that I have been secretly collecting a computer file of selected trivia pearls that you, my absent Mr. Boyd, put out on a daily basis. Hundreds of pieces of trivia. I plan to dip into the file from time to time like a box of hidden chocolates or love letters to rekindle my passion, before I begin my twelve-step program to break the habit of trivia dependency. Just so you'll know.

# Shelf Life

My mother-in-law used to say, whenever she was overcome by a deluge of cultural change she could not understand, that she had "lived too long." That remark was usually made when adult grandchildren grew facial hair or pinched bath towels from the Holiday Inn. I always thought it a strange thing to say. I was in my thirties and planned on living forever. Change was good. I thought all the world was in revolution . . . just the way it should be. And I figured my shelf life was endless.

Recently in Charleston, an elderly man sidled up to me and said he wanted to write a brief book to leave to his middle-aged children. His proposed book would impart his one central bit of grim wisdom, gleaned from eight decades of life experiences: Don't outlive your money. An idea born in the Depression, it is a frightening prospect, especially when coupled with the vagaries of old age. But is it the key message you want to leave your children?

Can you assure your own legacy? Maybe so. One man who outlived early incarnations of himself was that old Democrat-turned-Republican from South Carolina, Strom Thurmond. He celebrated his hundredth birthday six months before he died in 2003. The fact that Thurmond was born during the administration of Theodore Roosevelt, just thirty-seven years after Appomattox, while Mark Twain was still writing, is stunning.

Thurmond, the oldest member of the Senate, spent much of his last years checking into and out of hospitals. The senator said in an interview that he couldn't recall exactly why he was in the hospital the last few times. Eventually, he lived at Walter Reed Army Medical Center. One definite advantage of extreme old age is forgetfulness. He hadn't a clue that he was a permanent resident.

Thurmond was governor when I was in grammar school in Columbia, South Carolina. At that time, a photograph of the forty-year-old governor standing on his head to court his first wife was published in *Life* magazine; it remains an image indelibly inscribed on my brain. The name Thurmond was a cuss word in our household. It was usually coupled with adjectives like "yellow-bellied" and similes such as "crooked as a dog's hind leg." In our family, it had to do with Thurmond's political takeover of the state forestry department. It was up close and personal.

Thirty years later, when I returned to South Carolina after a lengthy absence, I was amazed to hear Thurmond's name spoken in reverential terms. He had reinvented himself. Longevity had transformed the opportunistic Dixiecrat of the 1940s into a dignified Republican senior statesman in the 1970s.

If you live long enough, will you be awarded the title of crone or sage just because you have survived your detractors and their recollections of your misdeeds? Does it mean that the population in general has a short memory and that details of the past, unsavory or not, will eventually be lost in America's collective brain?

Not in Thurmond's case. He must have thought he was home free, if he was even able to consider that at the end. The disclosure of the existence of Strom Thurmond's biracial daughter after his death was a bombshell to many, but apparently not to some South Carolinians, who had heard rumors for years. The revelation that a twenty-two-year-old Thurmond had fathered the child of a fifteen-year-old who worked in his parents' house put yet another twist on the elder-statesman image. Thurmond's history had taken an eleventh-hour turn. He was recycled, all right, but by someone else this time. His place in history is secure, but as what?

It does make you wonder about your own shelf life. For some, it seems that their deeds and stories live on. Wilmington artist Claude Howell's work is a beloved mainstay at the Louise Wells Cameron Art Museum. Though he has been gone many years, Claude still tells stories in that memorable voice on WHQR Public Radio, thanks to his taped commentaries. A voice from the grave.

You might want to hurry up and record those old family anecdotes and stories real soon. Label the backs of all photographs. They will be part of your legacy. Don't wait. Like that old container of peach yogurt in the fridge, your expiration date may have already come and gone.

# Sign Language

Growing up in the era of the ubiquitous Burma Shave signs, I quickly became a devotee of "sign language." Spotting Burma Shave signs on road trips was eminently more satisfactory than playing cow poker, in which you counted cows on your side of the road until your score was wiped out when you passed a graveyard. Somehow, your sister always managed to sit on the side of the car that passed a sea of cows and no graveyards.

The fifties were the heyday of the Burma Shave marketing revolution, which lasted from 1925 to 1963. Not a bad run for a scheme that catapulted a small, brushless shaving cream into advertising history. Where else could you find such deathless poetry?

Altho insured
Remember kiddo
They don't pay you
They pay your widow
Burma Shave

Or

Dinah doesn't
Treat him right
But if he'd shave
Dina-mite
Burma Shave

Or my all-time favorite:

My job is
Keeping faces clean
And nobody knows
De stubble I've seen
Burma Shave

Interstates and freeways have made the clever Burma Shave five-sign tour de force as obsolete as the running board, so I've had to look for an alternative fix for road reading. This can be done on Southern back roads and in towns where Protestant churches—mostly Baptist and Methodist—have taken to using marquees to get their messages to the people. Small towns are especially good for this. The Bible Belt has a real flair for epigrammatic wit.

Where do these sign ideas come from? Word is that there is an actual book of brief ecclesiastical marquee messages out there. And the Internet is a ready source. I found one favorite: "Seeking a sign from God? This is it." And a clever one: "This is a ch _ _ ch. What is missing?"

Okay, I'll give you a minute to think about that one.

Some churches have parishioners who dream up original messages. The Hartwells at Masonboro Baptist Church have been the authors of their church marquee for years now. They think up most messages and "borrow" others. Pastor Gordon Wright says laughingly that some even have to be censored.

Their latest effort: "We have better news for you. You can save more with God than Geico."

On Oleander Drive, one church sign seemed especially appropriate for our ocean-side town: "You want to walk on water? You've got to get out of the boat."

Also on Oleander Drive, from the Methodists: "God answers knee-mail."

A trip to Myrtle Beach revealed, "Stop, drop, and roll doesn't work in Hell."

From an Elizabethtown funeral home, this reassuring billboard: "We'll be the last ones to let you down."

The week after Hurricane Isabel, I saw this on the way to Fayetteville, near Roseboro: "Storms in your life . . . ask Jesus." On the same trip, I spotted, "Flying lessons still offered. Inquire within" and "Life has many choices, eternity but two." I like the companion piece to that: "How will you spend eternity? Smoking or non-smoking?" I rolled on by the Joyful Noise Nursery School and passed Nirvana Lane as I left Roseboro. In the South, there is something for everyone.

Passing a country cemetery on the way to Swansboro, I stopped the car and snapped a photograph of an enormous pink plastic floral tribute in the shape of a princess telephone emblazoned with a banner that read, "Jesus called."

. Southerners are noted for their exceptional gift of language. Even in death, we like to have the last word.

# Ma'am

Poor Queen Elizabeth II. She has been called "ma'am" since she was twenty-four, for goodness' sake. I hated that when it happened to me in my forties, and I wasn't even the queen.

The woman worked hard for fifty years. She deserved a vacation. Queen Elizabeth II toured Canada with her rascally consort, Philip, on the last stop for her jubilee year. Hitting twelve cities in twelve days can hardly be deemed a vacation. (If it's Thursday, it must be Toronto.) But I must say the newspaper photos showed the old girl looking quite cheerful in her pastel coat, matching Bundt-cake hat, and the ever-present and ever-empty matching handbag dangling from the regal wrist.

These sorties from the palace must have added spice to her royal routine. One spring when the queen was on a grand tour, a resident of Newcastle jogged along beside her Rolls-Royce waving and shouting, "Yoo-hoo, yoo-hoo!" As the royal couple turned to respond, they realized he was buck-naked. The streaker circled and revealed his greeting, scrawled across his rear end. It read, "Rude Britannia."

If ever anybody needed a stretch of good road, it was the queen. Her *annus horribilis* stretched into a *decadus horribilis*: Fergie's toe-sucking episode; disturbing rumors of royal blame for the automobile wreck of Diana and Dodie; the burning of Windsor Castle; hubby's verbal blunders and rumored romantic escapades; Prince Harry's bout with weed and costume-party disaster; Paul Burrell, the light-fingered butler and confidant to Diana, hauled into court for the theft of Diana's peach Valentino evening gown and a bullwhip, a gift from Harrison Ford. (A wickedly intriguing pair of stolen items. What was that all about?)

The Camilla issue must have caused a facial tic for the queen mum, though Elizabeth was used to in-law dilemmas by that point in time. The queen's own mother-in-law, Princess Alice of Greece, took to wearing an all-black nun's habit back in the 1930s . . . despite the incongruous fact that she persisted in drinking and smoking. In 1947, the year of the royal wedding, she showed up at every prenup party for Elizabeth and Philip in her cheery black getup. The ensemble must have been a real icebreaker. The Windsors couldn't even throw a birdcage cover over her funereal robes. She was, after all, the royal MOG—mother of the groom. And you think your in-laws are difficult.

It's enough to make any woman whimper for more peaceful golden years and call for a royal Advil or at least a majestic martini. Besides having the most dysfunctional family outside of the Deep South, below are a few of the drawbacks of being queen.

No royal lounging outfits. No gold lamé sweats for frumping around the castle. No royal clam diggers or jeweled flip-flops for schlepping about the palace. Just tailored suits and good Scottish sensible shoes.

Bad pocketbooks. No Kate Spade or funky over-the-shoulder totes where you can stash your paperback book.

No water aerobics at the Y. Just the old girl bobbing alone in the palace pool in an imperial long-sleeved bathing suit with her tiara attached to her bathing cap. The queen is the poster child for fifties helmet hair and suffers, I am sure, from hat hair and crown hair as well.

I have a suspicion that Buckingham Palace harbors no Coke machines. I find this deeply depressing.

Since she has no girlfriends, there's no meeting the group for a dishy lunch. Even if there were girlfriends, what would Elizabeth have to dish except her own family?

On the other hand, there are perks to being the queen.

No car pools . . . ever.

No doctors' waiting rooms. She may be the only patient on the planet who remembers what the archaic term *house call* means.

No waiting for the electrician to show up or the dishwasher repairman to appear. Or the cable TV guy to drop in.

She must have her own platinum royal remote. No jockeying with her spouse for that TV necessity.

And of course, husband Philip always walks deferentially to the rear and left of her, something my husband has fantasies about my doing for years. And that's what that always will be . . . a fantasy.

But rule Britannia? No thanks, not even for a day.

# Two Degrees of Separation

John Guare's play *Six Degrees of Separation* was based on psychologist Stanley Milgram's "small-world phenomenon." The 1967 theory stated that every single person on earth is connected by links . . . with only six links (at most) necessary to join any two people in the world. A parlor game and eventually a board game, developed with the premise that everybody in Hollywood is connected to Kevin Bacon, became hugely popular.

This is a terrific mind game, and essentially very Southern. We've always loved to link folks, even non-family. Take George Bush. Connection: My daughter went to a reception and met President Reagan in Raleigh in the 1980s. Reagan knew the Bushes, both senior (as V.P.) and junior. So that put me three degrees from senior and four from Dubya. Charles, the prince of Wales, spoke on the parade ground at the Citadel in the 1970s, when Ernie, my husband, was provost marshal at the school, and we were on the dais with him. That made us two degrees from the queen mum, three from Princess Di, and four from John Travolta (remember that dance at the White House?). The first opera I ever saw was *La Boheme* with Renata Tebaldi singing Mimi. Since she and Maria Callas were rivals and had met on several occasions, that made me three degrees from Maria's lover, Aristotle Onassis, and four from his wife, Jackie O.

I've always loved North Carolinian Ava Gardner, that radiant cinematic image (I hesitate to call her an actress). Mama always said Ava was the most beautiful woman in Hollywood, and that was because she was Southern. Mama was a bit of a xenophobe. I don't know that I see a cause-and-effect relationship, but there is no denying Ava's drop-dead looks.

In *My Forbidden Past* with Robert Mitchum (we always called him "Sleepy" Mitchum), an old black-and-white flick that Howard Hughes apparently set up for Ava as a token of his friendship, her luminous face was spectacular. The film *The Aviator* depicts the earthy Smithfield beauty as the friend who took a no-nonsense approach to Hughes's uber-weirdness. From all reports, he appreciated and respected her no-frills friendship.

I have traced the degrees of separation to the beauty from Grabtown. When I was at Chapel Hill, I dated a Sigma Chi. (Or was he a PiKA? For the life of me, I can't remember which.) We were often at the fraternity house. In the powder room downstairs, a toilet seat hung on the wall as a decorative element. A small beribboned sign beneath the seat said, "Ava Gardner sat here!" Now, if that sign were gospel, it puts me only two degrees from Ava Gardner and three from Howard Hughes. And who needs Kevin Bacon when you have Howard Hughes? Game on.

# Memory Bank

Mama's earliest memory, she always said, was of being bundled in a blanket one cool spring evening in 1910 and being carried by her father out on an Alabama hillside to watch Halley's comet streak across the sky. "Remember this night," she was told. "You are seeing a sight that no one will see again for another seventy-six years." She was told about the night the shower of stars fell on Alabama back in 1833. People all over the state thought the meteor shower signaled the end of the world.

Mama's detailed account of seeing Halley's comet makes her among the most precocious of three-year-olds. A small technicality. Southerners never let the facts get in the way of a good story.

Born forty-two years after the Civil War, Mama had a vivid sense of the war and its tragic circumstances, garnered from accounts of the older adults in her life. We always had the sense of the "Wah" as a recent event, even when I was growing up.

Allan Gurganus, North Carolina author of *Oldest Living Confederate Widow Tells All*, recounts an anecdote that reflects both the awe of the past and the confusion about particulars. A father living in Richmond, Virginia, began an annual rite of taking his young son down to Monument Avenue overlooking the center of Richmond, to visit the huge bronze statue of General Lee astride his famous horse Traveller. The two would stand beneath the monument while the father recounted the virtues of General Lee, the greatest hero of the War of Northern Aggression. On and on he droned, detailing battlefield heroics, campaign strategies, and the courage, the gentility, and the character of Robert E. Lee. By the time the boy was nine, he was familiar with every detail, since he heard the same litany every year.

The following year on the pilgrimage, the son again listened patiently. When his father finished, he turned to the boy.

"Son, do you understand why it is important that you know about General Lee and what he did for the South?"

"Yes, Daddy, I do understand," said the boy. "But I do have one question. Who is that *man* riding on General Lee?"

Understanding may come years after a significant historical event. I witnessed a race riot when Arthurine Lucy made the first attempt to integrate the University of Alabama and Governor George Wallace came to turn her away. For three days, I saw mobs careening across campus in what started as a panty raid and ended up a full-fledged riot with cars overturned and general vandalism. The TV cameras of the world focused on Tuscaloosa. The next year, I transferred to the University of North Carolina at Chapel Hill.

What did I learn from seeing the race riot? That mobs are ugly and frightening. That I was politically naive, unaware of most social issues. That I hoped a better day was coming for us all, black and white. That my education was important to me. That I wanted to be more than what I laughingly called a PSB— a Professional Southern Belle.

Memory defines who we were, who we are, and who we hope to be. Tape-record your uncle telling of his World War II experience. Ask your grandmother about the Great Depression. Write down your sister's recollections of Elvis mania in the fifties. Do it for yourself. Do it for your family. You won't be sorry.

# Suits Me

The decision to take up water aerobics presented a major problem: the bathing suit. I had not purchased a suit since 1983, when I hit the big sale at Thalheimer's and bought two at a 75 percent off sale. Those suits saw water only a couple of times in the eighties but were too good to relegate to the Salvation Army, so they have survived two moves and two decades since they left the relative calm of Thalheimer's, which bit the dust long before the suits did.

When I pulled the swimsuits from the back of the closet, I noticed that, though the fabric was dated and a bit tired looking, the highly structured bustlines were as perky today as they were many years ago. Those were the days when *natural* was not even in the swimsuit vocabulary. The suits were throwbacks to the engineering expertise resulting from Howard Hughes's fixation on Jane Russell's bustline in the notorious movie *The Outlaw*, which I wasn't allowed to see at the time. Remarkable. My bathing suits' upper-body infrastructure was so intact that they could easily have gone out on dates without benefit of a human body inside.

Fearful that the aging suits might disintegrate when the water hit them, as the Wicked Witch of the West did in *The Wizard of Oz*, I nixed them. They went back to the closet, probably accepting dates with those madras Bermuda shorts six hangers down, which my husband last wore to a picnic in 1978.

I needed an acceptable twenty-first-century model for an antique swimmer. Once in the swimsuit department, I began to feel as if I were shopping for a troll. My requirements for the suit were legion. Let's see . . . a dust ruffle to disguise cellulite, wide straps to conceal as much flesh as possible, a dark, solid color (the large girl's best friend), the slenderizing leg style euphemistically called "little boy legs." Finding just the right suit was a large order, pun intended.

I actually found two bathing suits on sale. I am beginning to believe these large-size suits travel only in pairs, like homely girls at a party. One suit was a real surprise. I tried to overlook the fact that it had a breastplate of a pewterlike metal the size of a half dollar, on which the mysterious initials DB were emblazoned. I did not realize until later that the suit was from that defunct Southern designer Suzanne Sugarbaker, a.k.a. Delta Burke.

But the real revelation unfolded when the water aerobics class started and I donned the suit and actually went in the pool. The unbelted skirt, which I figured was a plus, floated to the surface of the water and remained there for the duration of the class, like a large, dark algae bloom on a pond. Even worse, I realized that Delta, in some misguided attempt to transform her customers into Southern belles, had made the underpinnings of the suit out of flesh-colored net and black material. The skimpy black material, although attached to the flesh-colored net, looked like a mock bikini from a distance of several feet. Talk about a sick joke. I am now convinced that Delta is a sadist out to inflict cruel and unusual punishment on any spectator within shouting distance of the faux bikini. Now, I ask you, is that any way for one nice Southern belle of a certain age to treat another?

The Delta suit, after months of heavy-duty chlorine, has begun to sag in places that I don't. It's time for another of my dreaded swimsuit searches.

# Water World

The characters that inhabit my 7:45 A.M. water aerobics class at the Y are as varied and strange as the denizens of the deep. Their names I don't know, but we are all speaking acquaintances.

"The Ancient Mariner" is a hardy octogenarian who is a regular. He meanders into the pool area wearing a dark Speedo and weights strapped to his ankles with huge rubber bands. He waves vigorously to the entire aerobics class. We all wave back. It is a ritual. He waits until everybody in the class has responded. If we do not wave back, he will stand there waving forever.

Several regular lap swimmers are very vocal—"the Grunters," I call them. Every four or five strokes, they let loose a mighty "Unhhh." You soon develop a nervous tic, swiveling your head to check the Grunter to make sure the "Unhhh" was not a final gasp. So far, so good.

There is ongoing discord between the lap swimmers and the water aerobics folk. The lap swimmers disdain us as dilettantes unworthy of pool space. They feel we're not really serious swimmers. Some lap folk take to cannonballing into the water to see if they can rattle "the Aerobics," who sport fifties, helmet-style, well-lacquered hairdos that do not take kindly to moisture in any form. Some members of the class have taken to wearing shower caps that recall those old refrigerator container covers for leftovers, before the advent of Tupperware. It is not a good look fashion-wise, but we have long abandoned couture for practicality.

My favorite character I call "the Snorkeler." She appears at the swim lane in her standard attire: full-size Jacques Cousteau black flippers, heavy-duty goggles, webbed gloves, and a snorkel tube for breathing. Having never seen her out of costume, I don't have a clue about her age or actual appearance. She lowers herself into the heavily chlorinated water and snorkels slowly to the other end of the pool, intently searching for some lost Atlantis on the cement bottom. Then she repeats the process again and again. Aside from an occasional run-in with the plastic lane separators, her search for the lost and the undiscovered continues.

We miss "Bob the Sinker," one colorful classmate who took off from the Y class for the summer to swim in his neighborhood pool. Bob had a weight-distribution issue that made him buoyancy challenged. Even with a flotation belt, he was always submerged up to his nostrils. He also developed a decided starboard list as the class wore on.

The rest of us in the water aerobics class float languidly, like so many Chinese dumplings in a sea of chlorinated broth. Sometimes, I think of us as an acre of cellulite, but I'm basing that on my own particular character flaw.

Water aerobics is a forgiving exercise. If you goof in technique, no one sees your underwater error. So we're a cheerful and peaceful group, aside from a few territorial issues about who is in your spot in the shallow end, a problem I understand also arises amongst regular gym folk and land aerobics classes. Under instructor Ann's ever-sunny guidance, we stretch, flex, jog, cross-country ski, and do frog jumps and jumping jacks, as agile as trained seals. Looking like the boy astride the dolphin on the ancient Greek coin, we ride our colorful Styrofoam noodles the length of the pool. I learned from the physical therapist at rehab that the exercise noodle is officially called a "woggle." That must be the medical term.

We make small jokes about exercises specifically designed to work on the abs or the waist.

"This is an excellent move for the waist," the instructor says.

"The waist? Yeah, I think I used to have one of those," someone will crack, and the dumplings all chuckle.

I've got to go now. I wouldn't want to miss a single minute at the pool.

# Mandarin for "Friend"

The Chinese restaurant Szechuan 132 is one of our favorites. It serves delicious food, and the iced tea is simply the best in town. This from a lifelong Southerner is high praise indeed. I am a highly qualified judge of grits and iced tea. Grits at Szechuan would be hard to come by, but the iced tea . . . oh my!

My son, Howell, was a regular at Joe's and introduced us to the owner. Joe is the only person on the planet Howell allows to call him "Howard."

Joseph Hou, owner of Szechuan 132, is so personable he makes Dale Carnegie look like a rank amateur. His customers get more than moo goo gai pan. They bask in the unique hospitality of the owner, who knows just about everybody who comes in his restaurant by name. Table by table, shaking hands, he works the clientele like a consummate pro. The names of your grandchildren, upcoming boat trips, your son's graduation—every guest has a personal exchange and feels that, somehow, he has made Joe's day. He is the ultimate Chinese schmoozer. Correction, he is the ultimate schmoozer.

"Joe, you should be running for something. Maybe a career in politics," I casually mentioned to him one day.

He replied with exquisite Oriental irony, "Politics? That's not my cup of coffee."

Joe is from India. He tells me his hometown, Calcutta, is no longer called "the Black Hole," as I had always heard growing up. According to Joe, it is now "the City of Joy." He left the City of Joy for the City That Never Sleeps, staying in New York some years before coming to Wilmington, North Carolina, in 1988 and opening his restaurant. He tells me that his people were originally from *southern* China. Why am I not surprised? He is a Southerner both by heritage and by choice.

Joe has more nephews and nieces than most native-born Southerners, and that's saying something. A Southerner can turn over a rock and unearth a cousin once removed. Joe's numerous nieces and nephews apprentice as waitpeople at his restaurant until they are launched into the world outside of Joe's protective umbrella.

Some years back, our son had just gotten out of three days in intensive care after a double lung transplant operation and was back in his room in the transplant wing at Chapel Hill Memorial Hospital. We looked up to see Joe standing in the doorway with yet another nephew, who had arrived in this country the day before. Joe had come from Wilmington to Chapel Hill to visit, bringing small containers of kung pao chicken, egg drop soup, and spring rolls as a get-well gift. Joe's nephew watched silently. It must have been a curious initiation into the Western world. You can keep your chicken soup. Egg drop soup is a miracle cure all its own.

Joe always tells me that when he is feeling low, he thinks about that day at the hospital when Howell, only three days out from his operation, insisted Joe walk with him down the corridor as he slowly pushed his assorted IV poles and paraphernalia beside him. Joe says whenever he thinks about Howell that day, his dark mood vanishes. How can he complain? he says.

I have learned many things from Joe since I've known him, but only a single phrase in Mandarin, and that is *paong yow*: friend.

# The Nobel Prize for Next-to-Nothing

They handed out the Nobel Prizes recently. I'm really most interested in the one for literature, which hasn't been announced, and the big kahuna, the Nobel Peace Prize.

I like to meditate on prizes I would give out to the forgotten souls who have made small but significant differences in my life. If I had the wherewithal to present a million dollars to these folks, I would. Or at least gift certificates to the local pizzeria.

I would give a prize to the inventor of hair spray, though I am sure he made a very good living at the glue factory before he started fiddling around with aerosol cans and shellac. Dolly Parton, the patron saint of hair spray, would be the appropriate presenter.

Hair spray has changed the lives of all of us out here with fifties hair. High-maintenance pompadours and spit curls were a mere dream before we had the propelled emulsion that could stay the "do" through a tsunami.

Ever-versatile hair spray also comes in handy when water bugs, as we so delicately call them—cockroaches in less southerly climes—wander in unexpectedly and you are out of Black Flag. A shot of White Rain or VO5 spray will stop the little suckers in their tracks as if they've been caught playing the old children's game of sling the statue. They are frozen in an armor of hair spray, little legs and antennae permanently suspended in midair, an insect cryogenic experiment. It does give you pause to see the effect on the insects' nervous systems and realize that we spray the very same substance a quarter-inch over our brains on a regular basis. Hair spray will also remove pesky ballpoint-pen ink from your shirt . . . if you wash it a million times until the ink and the color of the garment disappear.

Post-it notes rank high on my list of stellar inventions, nudging hair spray as a top contender. The little stickers adorn every book I own, cover the screen of my computer with operational instructions, and plaster the fridge with reminders of when I am supposed to be where. I'm especially partial to those in brilliant dayglow colors, so visually arresting that an array of them can give you a migraine. I even find them on my clothes from time to time, stuck to my sleeve or the hem of my dress. They take on a life of their own, following me like a bad reputation, showing up months after their timeliness has vanished. I like to think of them as remnants of an archaeological dig of my past appointments and transitory concerns.

My OXO vegetable peeler is on the list. It *must* be an OXO brand, with the big rubber handle. Peeling a carrot or a potato with an OXO transforms a chore into a spiritual experience. I gave an OXO to my daughter. A second-generation punster, she allowed that "it works just fine, but it does not make the cut to the life-changing category." It must be a geezer thing.

Velcro is a winner. My granddaughter's shoes all have Velcro straps instead of shoelaces. I personally believe a woman must have invented this marvel. All doll clothes are now made with Velcro fasteners instead of those dad-blamed teeny buttons. I feel strongly that Velcro makes our little girls more serene and more centered at play and is essential for developing a confident can-do attitude.

Honorable mentions: Sharpie felt markers, the undo button in the task bar of my computer, and the retractable dog leash.

You probably have your own Nobel Prizes to give out. The best part is, you won't even have to go to Stockholm.

# Like the Cracker

Because of my Southern accent, sometimes people I'm introducing myself to think I am saying "Brown" rather than "Graham." I usually correct them by saying, "No, it's Graham, like the cracker."

Everybody knows that ubiquitous snack from childhood. But who was the Graham after whom the healthful cookie was named? A nineteenth-century health guru named Sylvester Graham who, after failing to make a go at saving souls as a Presbyterian minister, resolved to save America's bodies by employing his trinity of good health: sexual moderation, exercise, and proper diet.

The New Englander covered the Northeast giving lectures on the health benefits of sexual abstinence and vegetarianism. He railed against feather beds, alcoholic beverages, coffee, tea, tobacco, tight corsets, and all meat in particular. All condiments must be eliminated from meals, since mustard and ketchup caused insanity, the diet evangelist proclaimed. Only three meals a day, precisely six hours apart, were permitted.

His followers, called "Grahamites," flocked to hotels, board-inghouses (known as Graham Houses), and restaurants around the country that featured menus of his recommended vegetarian cuisine. In the 1840s, Oberlin College even put its entire student body and faculty on the Graham diet of water and graham crackers for several months . . . until the roar of student protest began to drown out the voices of the lecturing professors.

Graham's elimination of meat in the diet was key. Meat caused epilepsy, insanity, and, at the least, headaches. Worst of all, it promoted lust, which brought on ill health. Since he believed that sex caused disease, he advised his disciples "to marry, get the urge out of their systems and let it fade." Sex for married couples was to be limited to no more than a tidy twelve times per year.

His diet, built around the mainstay of his own graham bread or crackers, promised to reduce sexual desire and, with any luck, eliminate it altogether. Graham's regimen would turn the body into a robust and fit machine. His well-attended lectures took on a revivalist fervor. There were thousands of converts at each event. The lectures proved so controversial that women fainted by the dozens (or pretended to) on hearing his revolutionary sexual agenda.

Ten years after the introduction of his whole-grain cracker, he changed his strategy, eliminated the focus on sex, and concentrated on nutrition. Controversy still raged. At his lectures in Boston, riots broke out among butchers and bakers protesting the self-proclaimed health sage. After all, vegetarianism and home-baked graham bread were economically devastating to bakers and butchers. City dwellers would not need their services. It was downright un-American.

No walking advertisement for his own theories, Graham's health declined dramatically in his early fifties. Debilitated, unable to walk, he died alone at fifty-eight despite his diet and a barrage of remedies that failed him when he needed them most. The health czar was a broken man, a laughingstock among his neighbors, a crackpot to the world at large. Grahamites faded into oblivion.

If you think you are eating the real thing when you eat a graham cracker, think again. Word has it that today the crackers are concocted from white flour instead of the graham flour so wildly lauded for better than a century and a half.

But Graham was not all crackers. He advocated bathing at least three times a week, back in the days when bi-monthly cleansing was customary. He insisted teeth should be brushed every single day whether they needed it or not, again a radical notion in the nineteenth century. He advocated seven hours of sleep every night, fresh fruits and vegetables, and plenty of exercise. Too bad it didn't work out for him personally. It must have been the sex thing.

Now, if people ask "Brown?" when I garble my last name, I won't say, "Graham, like the cracker." I think I'll go with "No, Graham, like the evangelist. Cud'n Billy, that is."

# Toga Ken

I've had two Ken incidents. That's Ken, boyfriend of the
Barbie doll. Barbie is past age forty-five but was in step with the
trend toward younger boyfriends years ago. Ken is two years
younger. I hear the two have parted company. Ken was unceremoniously dumped. Two years younger didn't cut it with Barbie
anymore.

My granddaughter, Caroline, once bought a Ken doll at a
garage sale. Unfortunately, Ken was nekkid, as we say down
South, which may account for his bargain price of twenty-five
cents. On returning home, Caroline discovered that Ken could
not wear Barbie's slacks or shorts. Ken apparently has wider hips
than Barbie. Go figure.

Molly, my inventive daughter, came up with the idea of a
toga for Ken, since she had a handkerchief and a piece of ribbon
handy and, like her mother, limited seamstress skills. Thus was
created Toga Ken. Skeptical Caroline wanted the toga explained.
Molly dragged out photos from her seventh-grade Latin Conference at the College of Charleston. Molly's homemade toga en-

semble for the conference was quite something, if I do say so myself. A peach brushed-cotton chiton with a darker peach toga, it was not nearly as nerdy as it sounds. Posed against the Doric columns of a Neoclassical building at the college, Molly looked very much the Roman.

Caroline even toyed with the idea of a toga party for her next birthday, an interesting idea when you think of the usual pool party, gym party, Spider-Man party, and so on. I could envision tiny little folk in togas, laurel wreaths, and sandals drinking Hawaiian punch out of plastic goblets and lounging on yoga mats. Maybe a film for the kids? Question is, would you say *Animal House* with John Belushi is appropriate fare for five-going-on-six-year-olds? Nah.

A few days later, I read about Fashion Insider Ken in the *New York Times*. Fashion Insider Ken looks like a poor man's Hugh Grant. Complete with poorly tailored suit, Hugh's signature tousled hair, and heavy-rimmed glasses, he is the newest Ken on the market.

I was curious about Ken. He didn't look anything like the GI Joe from my son's heyday. I learned that Ken has a last name: Carson. (Does that mean he has cousins Johnny, Kit, and Rachel?) I learned there is a wide, wide world of Kens, including Talking Ken in English and Talking Ken in Spanish.

There are Location Kens: Miami Ken, Sparkle Beach Ken, Surf City Ken, Rio de Janeiro Ken, Palm Beach Ken.

There are Apostrophe Kens (like Southerners, they always drop the final *g*): Sea Lovin' Ken, Sun Lovin' Malibu Ken, Animal Lovin' Ken, Cool Shavin' Ken, Cool Lookin' Ken, Horse Lovin' Ken.

The popular Activity Kens reflect the changing times: Movie Date Ken, Disco Ken, Safari Ken, Nature Adventure Ken, Concert Date Ken, Tennis Ken, Jogging Ken, Ski Fun Ken, In-Line Skating Ken.

Then there are the Ken Your-Mama-Wouldn't-Let-You-Date Kens: Party Time Ken, Rappin' Rockin' Ken, Wet 'n Wild Ken,

Free Movin' Ken, Harley-Davidson Ken, Beach Blast Ken, Sensational Malibu Ken, Hot Rockin' Fun Ken.

There are Professional Kens. These are few and far between. Our hero usually prefers to hang out as Beach Fun Lovin', G-Droppin' Ken. Doctor Ken, who is a pediatrician, comes with little outpatient Tommy. There's also Olympic U.S. Skater Ken, Stars & Stripes Air Force Ken, Thunderbird Ken, Stars & Stripes Marine Ken, and Stars & Stripes Rendezvous with Destiny Army Ken. How did the army pull off that dramatic title?

There are Hair and Shavin' Kens. Popular culture's continuing obsession with hair is reflected in Cool Shavin' Ken, Shave 'n Style Ken, Shaving Fun Ken, Painted Hair Ken, Painted Hair Shortie Ken, Mod Hair Ken, Hollywood Hair Ken, and Sport & Shave Ken.

There are Hollywood Legend Kens: Cowardly Lion Ken, Scarecrow Ken, Tin Man Ken, Rhett Butler Ken, Henry Higgins Ken, Elvis in Gold Lamé Ken.

And the strangest Kens? Coca-Cola Ken, Day to Night Ken, Perfume Giving Ken, Butterfly Art Ken, Flower Surprise Ken, Modern Circle Ken, Earring Magic Ken. I did find out that Earring Magic Ken is a gay Ken with two-tone hair, a lilac mesh shirt, and a vinyl faux-leather vest. The rest? I haven't a clue.

My personal favorite is Walk Lively Ken. I presume this Ken is designed for senior citizens in their second childhood, with a silver walker as an accouterment.

A hundred years from now, when archaeologists dig up a Ken collection from some urban excavation site, what curious conclusions will they draw about the twenty-first-century male?

# *True Colors*


Every woman treasures key people in her life . . . aside from husband, children, and family, of course. There's Kathy at the dry cleaner's, who understands your wool and silk issues and always makes them right. Your gynecologist. God forbid you move and have to start that search over again. It's more daunting than selecting a husband. But highest on the list of essential beings is your hairdresser.

I belong to a generation that has taken a vow never to go gray. Most of us can't even recall our original hair color. Our husbands seem blithely unaware of our diligence in maintaining this façade of youth.

When we first moved to Raleigh from Charleston, I traveled 280 miles south every six weeks to my hairdresser, Sammy, for a fix. He was an eccentric who watched *Guiding Light* every day in the salon. I remember the day Roger Thorpe died and we clients cheered his villainous end. Sammy collected tacky souvenirs, the tackier the better. He had a wealth of *objets d'art*: hula dancers in seashells, a life-size rooster made from corn kernels, a plaster of

Paris lighted cactus that doubled as a nightlight and an earring holder. It was an incredible collection, each object more tasteless than the last. I've never known anyone else with that hobby. I think it was one of the reasons I kept going back to him. But I realized that a five-hour drive to my beauty salon and the connoisseur of kitsch was a bit excessive.

My current hairdresser runs her salon with blinding efficiency. Norma will not tolerate my calling it a "beauty parlor," as I did growing up. I am not allowed to say "dye" either. It's "color" or "tint," please. Norma makes the Prussian military look like the last of the lotus-eaters. I would rather be late for my own funeral than waltz in tardy for my cut or color.

We customers affectionately call Norma "the Normanator," "the Hair Nazi" being too extreme. She is wonderfully forthright. You always know where you stand with Norma. Like a sympathetic best friend, she dishes out beauty advice you sometimes would rather avoid.

Eyebrows, for instance. When they start to go gray (and they will), steps must be taken to return them to an acceptable color. What you want is something matching your hair that, naturally (well, not naturally, of course), will never turn gray. Taming unruly eyebrows is a specialty with Norma, who manages to keep you from looking like the runner-up in the Frida Kahlo Look-Alike Contest or long-ago labor leader John L. Lewis, who some of you might be old enough to remember. My wild eyebrows have taken on a life of their own. Unfortunately, their life is more interesting than mine.

I did not realize that I had evolved into a redhead until a friend mentioned it. I'm not talking Belle Watling red, which I did try my sophomore year in college, when I was feeling particularly rebellious. And anything is better than the waitress black I chose one summer after graduation, an unfortunate color that made my "do" bear no resemblance to human hair.

One redhead incarnation turned out to be a shade of plum. In my burgundy workout suit, I resembled a monster eggplant . . .

not a good look. Today, I'm a brownish red. Tahitian Sunset is my new hair color. I rather like being red in my golden years, though one woman at a book signing felt otherwise. "You sound blond on the radio," she said accusingly. I hate that I was such a disappointment. I guess most mature ladies do tend to go blond as they age. It just never appealed to me.

In the world of mousses, gels, sprays, lotions, and clarifiers, I'm happy to sit back, close my eyes, and inhale the rich, fruity fragrance that always seems to accompany a visit to Norma. It is like a trip to the tropics. I love to emerge smelling like a giant mango, walking tall amongst all of us redheads out there. It gives me an unbearable lightness of being.

# Wall to Wal-Mart

I turned off Market Street to pop into Wal-Mart for a bag of kitty litter on my way home from my water aerobics class at the Y the other week. Maybe it was chlorine fumes that made me do such a thing. For whatever reason, I turned into the parking lot without a clue that it was the very morning of the grand opening for the superstore.

I cruised through the rows of cars looking for an asphalt space amid the crush of humanity that had come out to celebrate the event. I finally beat out a Kathy Bates look-alike, snagged a parking spot several thousand yards from the store, and hiked to the entrance, which was ringed by policemen who were there, I assume, for riot control.

Wandering into the grocery section, I heard a bell—a cowbell, as it turned out. A seven-foot black-and-white cow with eyelashes Mae West would have killed for strolled among the frozen-food aisles. Occasionally, the Maola cow rang the bell around her neck and waved her hoof in a customer's face. She pranced and minced her way through the crowd. The sheer size of the animal suggested that the human within was a not a Bessie but a Buddy. If the inhabitant of the Maola suit were indeed male, he was a refugee from *Will & Grace*. He waved brightly as he skipped toward the produce aisle.

Exiting the food department, I turned into an aisle behind what I thought was the Pillsbury Doughboy. As he stopped and shook my hand, I saw it was not Poppin' Fresh at all but his first cousin once removed, the Michelin Man. The mushroom pallor and huge rolls of plasticized white stuff around his middle made me recognize the family resemblance. In fact, I had a flashback of my own image as I emerged from the dressing room suited up for my water aerobics class. I would have made a passable Michelin Man myself.

The loudspeaker announced in a breathless voice, "Shoppers, Ricky Rudd will be in the store from four to six this afternoon and will sign autographs for you at six sharp." I wondered if Ricky Rudd was another cartoon character from Madison Avenue. Only later did I find out he was a real NASCAR person and would not be appearing in an animal suit.

I finally found the Fresh Step kitty litter, which seemed to come only in the economy size. In lugging the huge pail toward the checkout, I elbowed the seven-foot, pink Energizer bunny from the line. The giant characters were starting to get on my nerves. The bunny, still pounding his drum, headed for housewares, rounding the bend at a toilet-brush display. I had the distinct feeling that I was an ancient Alice who had fallen into a huge neon rabbit hole.

The checkout girl, Tiffany, took my credit card from me after I made the twelfth swipe through the machine and the card would not process.

"I think it may have lost its magic," I said weakly.

She did not smile. She ran the card through over and over. She tried punching the numbers in manually. No luck. I wondered momentarily if my husband had cut off my plastic funds.

*213*

Tiffany closed her register, put on her flashing light to summon the supervisor, and waited.

Tiffany ended up taking an imprint by rubbing a large orange Crayola on a piece of paper over the credit card, the same technique used for a tombstone rubbing. She wrote the purchase amount on the back and put it in the cash drawer. So much for high tech.

Alice will not visit the rabbit hole in the near future. She is still recovering at home, having a Co-Cola with the Mad Hatter.

# Shopping 101

Men are excluded from this shopping analysis. Men do not like to shop. They do not understand the nuances of the profession. If they need something—say, a ball-peen hammer—they go to Home Depot and buy a ball-peen hammer. Now, I ask you, is that sporting? Does the vast array of ball-peen hammers out there have a chance with that kind of attitude? What about the cunning stainless-steel number that might be at Lowe's, or the fetching soft-grip-handle version that waits at Wal-Mart, or the fabulous iridescent Sears ball-peen aching to join the ratchets and bits in the toolbox? And you call yourselves sportsmen.

Women are born understanding the finer points of shopping. It is a gender-related virtue. It's in our DNA. We each have our own shopping modus operandi, as individual as our fingerprints.

I am what I designate a Presbyterian shopper. I see something I like—say, a sweater—and I examine it closely. I circle, go back, and look again. I don't really need it, but I want it. It is fabulous! But too pricey. But it *is* a great sweater. Wait. Is the color a shade too orange? Too fuchsia?

Another prospective buyer approaches. I feign indifference, knowing full well that any display of interest in the sweater will be like catnip to the other shopper. I watch sideways as she lifts my sweater and holds it up to her neck. I do not cave, and I do not buy the sweater. I leave the store.

I visit the red sweater several times during the next week. I establish a routine. I begin to use the personal pronoun . . . *my* red sweater. I agonize. Is it really right for me? Could I find a better one elsewhere? At a better price?

After several more trips to visit my sweater, my Calvinistic suffering is palpable. Though I long to purchase it, I wait for yet another week to go by. The next few days are delicious torture. Has someone else scarfed up my delectable sweater? Is it still there?

Anticipation hangs in the air like a haze as I enter the store. Will it be there, or will it be gone? If it is there, then I know it was meant to be *my* sweater. If it is gone, it was not meant to be. It was preordained to be someone else's sweater.

I had an eccentric great-aunt who shopped like a man. Everybody has a great-aunt who looks like my auntie, pronounced "ohn-tee" rather than "an-tee." A bit square-shaped, always in a dark crepe dress with a lace collar, D.A.R. bosom decked with a substantial brooch of colored glass. Her little, square feet were encased in sturdy shoes just one click short of orthopedic. She wore the same ones year-round: square-heeled Naturalizer lace-up shoes with perforated holes on each side of the laces. After buying her first pair in 1933 when she was fifty, she had purchased a new pair every five years since. The style never varied in the twenty years I knew her. Auntie was not one to be overwhelmed by the fickle winds of fashion.

Her visits to Tuscaloosa were her chance to go to our local department store, called Pizitz, for her Naturalizer outing. As a teenager, I was the designated driver for one such foray.

Though Auntie was a Presbyterian, she was not a Presbyterian shopper. As I mentioned, she shopped like a man. In the store, she ordered shoes identical to the ones she was wearing, tried them on, walked out to the sidewalk to view the footwear in the sunlight, walked up and down a bit in front of the store, and returned to the salesman.

"Well, Miz Morrow, how'd that pair do for you?" he smiled genially.

Auntie was all business.

"Just fine, Mr. Edwards. We'll take them."

She paid cash. The transaction was complete.

At home, she unwrapped the shoes to show Mama. She held them under the light and closely examined the soles.

"Well, I declare!" she cried. "Look, these shoes have been worn. That Mr. Edwards has sold me *used* shoes. Did you ever . . . !"

Auntie's hand fluttered over her collarbone, as if she were ready to swoon.

"You must take them right back and get me a brand-new pair," she said.

She was looking at me.

"But those scratches are from your walking up and down the sidewalk in front of the store," I protested.

Facing Mr. Edwards alone at Pizitz Department Store was one of my more mortifying teenage moments. It took me years to recover. But with therapy, I was able to return to the world of purchasing.

In my present-day Presbyterian shopping, suffering is key. It is a journey through a vale of tears. Auntie would be proud.

# Fowl Play

These are perilous times for the turkey, these weeks between Thanksgiving and Christmas. A recent exposé by ABC's John Stossel was upsetting, to say the least, and has raised my turkey consciousness to a new level. It seems that the Thanksgiving turkeys ceremoniously pardoned by the president in the Rose Garden of the White House have a dubious future. There are actually two presidential turkeys. The runner-up might be called upon to serve its nation should the chosen turkey for any reason be unable to perform its duties as presidential turkey.

And they have names. This Thanksgiving's names, Stars and Stripes, won out over Pumpkin and Cranberry. Last year's birds, Freedom and Liberty, hardly realized the irony in their names. Somehow, it seems that less-ambitious names—like Lincoln's Jack; the millennium turkey, Jerry; his vice turkey, Wallace; and their predecessors Harry and Troy—are more suitable for the emblematic birds.

As on Thanksgivings past, our national turkeys were released to a Virginia farm after the big day. Theoretically, Stars and Stripes are living the bucolic good life with unlimited freedom and food. But domesticated turkeys are so overweight and ill prepared to survive the real world that they live only for a couple of months after their fifteen minutes of fame before buying the farm, so to speak. Domesticated birds are sensitive in the extreme. They have such delicate sensibilities that they have been known to keel over when stressed by overhead jets and other unseemly noises. They are soothed by classical music but agitated by rock-and-roll, scientists tell us.

My empathy for the poultry is real. Today's noise-polluted world gives me the fantods, too. The turkey has a wattle (that fleshy drape under its chin) and a snood (the thing on top of its beak). These are terms I can relate to, since I am actually old enough to remember my aunts wearing their hair pulled back in snoods during World War II, and since I, a candidate for *Extreme Makeover*, also sport a wattle in these golden years.

But the wild turkey is a bird of a different feather. The turkey, the only native poultry in North America, was admired by Ben Franklin in its native state (the turkey's, not Ben's). Its life is a far cry from that of its domesticated brother.

In Alabama, turkeys are real turkeys—none of those steroid-enhanced, citified guys strutting around the Rose Garden. These wild birds can actually fly, unlike their city cousins. In Sumter County, turkeys are plentiful despite the popularity of hunting. Every truck has a gun rack in its rear window; mud flaps are covered with the real stuff; and every guy from toddler to teeterer wears camouflage. It is the alpha male's outfit du jour from early autumn through spring in these parts.

This past summer, I headed to our little tree farm to see if the hunters on the property had repaired the bridge and to check their hunting stands. Suddenly, we saw two preteen turkeys, known as "jakes," calmly standing side by side, waiting for our car to pass. I momentarily thought about calling them Mason and Dixon.

Several years ago, one avid deer hunter on the property

refused to leave his hunting perch in a hickory tree for Thanksgiving or Christmas. His wife and son dutifully came down for both holidays and huddled around the base of the tree beneath his deer stand, eating Vienna sausages out of the can and downing steaming coffee to keep the blood circulating in the sixteen-degree weather. And you thought Crazy in Alabama was just a movie starring Melanie Griffith.

We may not opt for a Christmas turkey this year. Maybe a goose. It's so Tiny Tim. Or perhaps a Vienna-sausage creation coaxed into the shape of a Christmas tree (with cherry tomatoes as ornaments), in honor of our Alabama hunter. Ummm, I'll get back to you on that.

# Relish the Day

We are having Christmas dinner away from home again this year. I'm really thankful when we are invited out and I am not the host for the feast. Given my limited culinary skills, it takes me a full twelve months of mental and spiritual rallying to get together a Christmas dinner. Plus, our messy house is piled high with essay papers to grade and stacks of Christmas presents to wrap.

I asked what I might bring to the dinner for ten people and was graciously waved off and told not to worry about it: "Just bring yourselves." But of course, my hostess is Southern, so I know she doesn't mean it when she says not to bring a thing.

I have checked with Roberts Market at Wrightsville Beach to see if the usual delights are available: sweet potato casserole, collards, stuffing. They are. Ambrosia is a possibility. But it's not available at Roberts, and I would rather be buggy-whipped than peel all that citrus. I have decided that I will devote my efforts this year toward an assortment of relishes and pickles.

I called my hostess to tell her this and got a puzzled response.

They already had some pickles they could put out, she said. There was an awkward silence. I realized she did not come from the relish tradition. No matter. Raised in a family in which pickles were considered as essential as salt and pepper, I will arrive at our host's home toting a satchel full of Southern specials.

I grew up where a holiday table was not complete unless it was groaning with pickles, relishes, and preserves of every description. The super-thin bread-and-butters were the mainstay. Those sweet, crisp cucumber delights, served chilled, were to us what the kosher dill is to Jersey—an essential. Another favorite was green-tomato pickles, mossy green medallions that rewarded the diner with the acid sunshine of the summer past.

My own children are partial to watermelon-rind pickles, a wonderfully sweet accompaniment that is first cousin to Southern sweet tea. The artichoke relish and pickles made from the Jerusalem artichoke, not the familiar globe artichoke, are my own first choice. I remember my mother-in-law making these in Goldsboro in the early days of my marriage. The Jerusalem artichoke looks very much like ginger root or ginseng, gnarled and twisted. Mamay used to take a sack full of dirty artichoke roots to the local Laundromat for a good scrubbing in a commercial Maytag, emptying the roots into the washing machine and feeding quarters into the slot. No one ever questioned her odd laundry load. She left with spotless artichokes ready to be cut and processed into delectable, gnarly whole pickles or finely chopped with red bell peppers into a mustardy artichoke relish.

Mama Dip's Kitchen in Chapel Hill, famous for Mama's soul food, understands the relish necessity. It always has a crock of homemade chow-chow right on the table, already there when you sit down. Chow-chow may challenge bread-and-butters as the ubiquitous side for the Southern table.

Pickled okra is a delight with its salty pungency. Writer Hal Crowther once said that okra, distinctly Southern, is like shrimp— nothing is wasted. With shrimp, you cut off the head and the tail, and the rest is all consumable. But when the okra is pickled, nothing is cut off. You eat the whole thing.

Visually spectacular, pickled peaches are a must at the holiday table. Those glistening golden globes of peachy flesh in sharply tart, sweet syrup look just right in a cut-glass bowl and add that necessary touch of Southern decadence to the meal.

So I wish you all a holiday of your favorite foods to be shared with your favorite people. And I hope you relish the day.

# Yes, Virginia

Word comes from Mexico City that anyone wearing red clothes and a white beard on the streets of the city will be arrested on the spot, presumably through December 25, to put impostors out of commission until the big day. This is not a ploy on the part of the Mythological Characters' Anti-Defamation League to eliminate jolly wannabes. It's the economy, stupid, as the T-shirts and politicians say.

It seems the gray market of Mexico, some 40 million street entrepreneurs, takes a bite out of the local merchants' Christmas profits, so in a singularly unseasonable spirit, authorities have banded together with Mexican scrooges to eliminate yuletide hucksters by unceremoniously hauling them off to spend the holidays in the hoosegow.

It's not the first time Santa has been down and out. The early European Saint Nick, based on the generous example of the Bishop of Myra, arrived not on December 25 but on December 6, coaxing an indolent donkey, rather than fanciful reindeer.

He left decidedly disappointing goodies like nuts, small clay figurines, and hard candies, according to author Charles Panini.

By the time of the Reformation, Saint Nicholas was generally banished from European countries, replaced by the more secular Father Christmas in England and Pere Noel in France. Neither was known as a lavish gift-giver, especially to children. Kiddies were not the focus of the universe at that point in history.

It was in America, of course, that Santa Claus developed a severe weight problem. In the 1880s, cartoonist Thomas Nast drew the fellow as we know him today—not as a slender, saintly bishop but as a roly-poly refugee from Jenny Craig.

And why do we still love this old guy even in the twenty-first century? Perhaps one of the reasons is that, in so many ways, as Pogo said, "he is us."

We're talking shortcomings here. Santa overindulges. His BMI is off the chart. His obesity makes us comfortable with our own girth as America adds inch after inch to its national circumference. Dr. Atkins heads up Santa's wretched-and-wrong list. Santa lives for cookies and cake. The missus reports his blood sugar is through the roof. A slave to his bad habits, the old guy sits on a curb outside his North Pole shop puffing away on that pipe, unable to smoke inside his own workplace under current OSHA regulations.

He is a chronic and natural-born snoop who loves to check up on everybody's behavior. He adores gossip about who has been naughty, just as we do. Santa is a lifelong subscriber to *People* magazine.

Santa always delegates tough jobs, like the construction of a zillion toys. Everybody knows who does the real labor. Those elves have no union, you know. Heaven forbid that anyone check into what the slave-driving boss benignly calls "Santa's Workshop," where the little folk labor for 364 days with no personal days, no paid vacation, no sick leave. Don't be fooled by those cunning little elf suits. They don't scream sweatshop, but you be the judge.

So Santa has many of our own faults. But the obese old elf also has our virtues. No one can fault him on generosity. He gives year after year, often receiving only lackluster thank-yous in return. He is tirelessly charitable with no thought of his own reward. He is selfless.

When it comes to delivering the goods, he is a one-man operation. There's no delegation of this chore. His work ethic is impeccable. He is dependable and reliable. He gets the job done in a timely manner. Despite the most severe weather and wildly hazardous driving conditions, he is relentlessly cheerful.

Finally, Santa represents the spirit of goodwill to every single one of his fellow men all over the world. He is the very best part of ourselves.

Nan Graham was born in Tallahassee, Florida, and grew up in Columbia, South Carolina, and Tuscaloosa, Alabama. She graduated from the University of North Carolina at Chapel Hill with an A.B. in English and received her M.A.T. in English from the Citadel in Charleston, South Carolina. Aside from her brief foray into the North after graduation, when she worked in New York City, she has lived her life in various parts of the South, and her books reflect her passion for things Southern.

She began her teaching career in Manhattan and has taught first grade, high school, and college; she currently teaches honors courses in Southern literature at the University of North Carolina at Wilmington. Graham has been a regular biweekly commentator for WHQR Public Radio in Wilmington since 1995. Her on-air tag line, "a lifelong Southerner," reveals the focus of her humorous commentaries on growing up and growing old in the South. Her first collection of radio essays, *Turn South at the Next Magnolia*, was on the SEBA bestseller list and was praised as "relentlessly Southern" by author Pat Conroy.

Graham has two grown children and a granddaughter. She lives in Wilmington with her husband, Ernie, a West Highland terrier named Grits, and Sumter, a semi-feral cat.